Kierkegaard As Theologian

Kierkegaard As Theologian

The Dialectic of Christian Existence

by Louis Dupré

SHEED AND WARD — NEW YORK

First published in Dutch under the title:
Kierkegaard's Theologie by De Standaard (Antwerp)
and Het Spectrum (Utrecht) 1958.

Library of Congress Catalog Card Number 63-8537

Manufactured in the United States of America

"To an unnamed . . ."
S.K.

CONTENTS

theologian in the Protestant or in the Catholic tradition? In
reading the many volumes of his diary one cannot but be
struck by his trenchant attacks on the Protestant Church,
and the apparent relation of many of his ideas with Catholic
doctrine. A closer investigation of his thought, however,
brought me to the conclusion that his *Existenzdialektik* is
perhaps the most consistent application of the Reformation
principle that has ever been made. Yet I think that this consistency makes his work a most valuable contribution to the
Catholic-Protestant dialogue.

One of the major problems of this dialogue is that the
partners do not understand each other, even though they
speak the same language. Kierkegaard's writings provide a
deeper insight into the religious impact of one of the basic
principles of the Reformation: the principle of subjectivity—
an insight which is sadly lacking among non-Protestants.
Even more important is the fact that for Kierkegaard, Christianity is a vital matter of the individual conscience and not a
social institution concerned primarily with respectability.
Protestants and Catholics object to Kierkegaard's religious
individualism. But he attracts both of them by his aversion
to the idea that Christianity is simply a stabilizing factor of
society, a significant ornament of Western civilization, or a
conservative force which can save modern man from losing
his identity in an impetuous world. In Kierkegaard all Christians face the dilemma that their religion is either all or
nothing, that it is true or false, and not true "to a certain
point." And this is a most refreshing experience in an epoch
which has given increasing importance to the psychological
and sociological effects of religion at the expense of its
transcendent content. Here is someone who takes Christianity's claims of transcendence seriously. Christians can be
united only on the basis of an authentic Christianity—a

watered-down ecumenism has no more religious meaning than a communion breakfast or a parish dance.

But there is more. With some of the conclusions he draws from the principles of the Reformation Kierkegaard rejoins the Catholic tradition. One of the most significant of these conclusions is the recognition of the role which freedom plays in the acceptance of faith and grace. Anxious to preserve God's transcendence against man's self-sufficiency, the sixteenth-century Reformers had all but eliminated this element, even though it is directly connected with the very principle of subjectivity. This matter will be discussed further in the chapters on faith and grace.

No less important is the reintegration of Christian asceticism in the *sola fide* doctrine of the Reformation. Although it is false that Luther eliminated the necessity of good works, he seems to be somewhat at a loss as to exactly where they fit in his doctrine of justification. This has led many of his followers, supported by their master's reaction against the Catholic theology of merit, to consider works as altogether superfluous. Coming from a Pietistic background and equipped with a more dialectical mind, Kierkegaard has been able to restore this essential part of the Christian tradition to Reformation theology. A special chapter on the Imitation of Christ will develop this in more detail.

Finally, in our concluding chapter we will take up the notion of authority. To many readers, Kierkegaard seems to defend a concept of authority as objective as that of papal infallibility. They conclude that he abandons the principle of subjectivity altogether and adopts the Catholic viewpoint. The fact of the matter is that Kierkegaard was never more consistently Protestant than on this particular point. He shows that subjectivity has a dialectic of its own which can lead to conclusions quite similar to those of a more objective theology. If Protestant theologians in the past had given the problem of authority more serious consideration, they would most likely have come to the same results.

It is precisely Kierkegaard's fidelity to his fundamentally Protestant convictions which constitutes his value for a dialogue between Catholicism and Reformation. His sharp dialectical mind has eliminated many fictitious problems which encumber the discussion about the real issues.

Yet this book is not an ecumenical study but an inquiry into Kierkegaard's own theology. What is Kierkegaard's theology? It certainly is not a system, and systematization risks losing the specific character of his thought. He considers himself as a Socrates in Christendom who, by his dialectical probings, brings modern man to reflect on Christian existence. Kierkegaard would have thought it the supreme irony of his life that sooner or later his attack on the system would itself be reduced to a system. And yet, even the best known commentaries[1] have not completely avoided this pitfall.

On the other hand, if Kierkegaard's thought is to be of universal value it must justify itself by its intrinsic necessity, independent of the circumstances of his personal life. But the difficulty is to discover this necessity. It seems to me that the German theologian and Kierkegaard scholar, Hermann Diem, has pioneered in this respect: he sees in Kierkegaard's existential experience the same intrinsic necessity which determines the dialectical development of Hegel's Idea. However, this position tends to reduce Kierkegaard's work to an "immanent" experience, and to neglect his profound "Christianity." True enough, Kierkegaard wanted to be a Socrates, but a Socrates *for Christians*. This means that his dialectic is not autonomous, but is at every moment determined by *transcendent* categories. The moments of his Christian dialec-

---

[1] Jean Wahl, *Etudes Kierkegaardiennes* (Paris, 1949); Thorsten Bohlin, *Kierkegaard's dogmatische Anschauung* (Gütersloh, 1927); and Martin Thust, *Kierkegaard, Der Dichter des Religiösen* (Munich, 1931).

tic do not follow an immanent necessity, but emerge from an existential experience of the transcendent.

If anyone object that such transcendence is still immanent in the sense that it is not concerned with the Transcendent itself, but rather with our still immanent relationship to it, I can only answer that it is with this very relationship that Kierkegaard is concerned. Whether a theology of the Transcendent *itself* is possible, is a question of capital importance in the philosophy of religion, but one which Kierkegaard does not treat. He describes only the dialectical relationship of the immanent with the Transcendent.

In the present study I shall follow this dialectic in a few central points. I have tried to present Kierkegaard's own ideas, not my ideas about Kierkegaard, and to refrain from all noninterpretative criticism. In the first chapter, however, on the relation between Kierkegaard's psychology and his religious ideas, I found myself compelled to adopt a personal viewpoint, since the question here is whether his near-pathological personality allows any autonomous interpretation of his work. It is only after having solved this preliminary question that we will be able to make an independent study of his religious thought. Of course, nowadays nobody would think of rejecting his work on purely psychological grounds, as some commentators did a few decades ago. Yet, we think that the psychographic approach has led to conclusions which a study of this sort cannot ignore. The first chapter will also give us the opportunity to state the necessary biographical data, with which the reader might not be familiar.

To conclude this introduction, I wish to express my special thanks to the Danish Ministry of Education, the Royal Library of Copenhagen, Dr. Niels Thulstrup, Secretary of the Kierkegaard Society in Copenhagen, and Dr. Richard Hansen of the Danish Institute in Brussels for their unstinting cooperation. I also acknowledge with special gratitude the invaluable assistance of Mr. William L. McBride, who re-drafted my own very rough English translation, of Dr. Germain Grisez and of Mr. Thomas Lane Anderson, who went over the whole text again. The extent to which my thought received adequate expression in English is due to their contributions. I must bear responsibility for whatever inadequacy remains.

SYSTEM OF REFERENCES

In quotations I always use the standard English translations where they exist, however questionable they might seem to some readers.

For the *Diary* I used *Søren Kierkegaards Papirer,* edited by P. A. Heiberg, V. Kuhr, and E. Torsting (Copenhagen, 1909-1948), 11 vols., in 20 parts.

Roman numerals indicate the volume; superscript Arabic numbers indicate the part, if a volume is divided into several parts. Letters A, B, or C stand for the section; Arabic numbers refer to the entry. For example: II A 11.

Wherever possible I used the partial translation by Alexander Dru of *The Journals* (New York, 1938), and refer to its entries by a second number in parentheses. For example: (X^2 A 481) (1061).

For the *Works* I used the second and last edition of *Samlede Vaerker,* edited by A. B. Drachmann, J. L. Heiberg, and H. O. Lange (Copenhagen, 1920-36).

In my list of abbreviations, the English titles of individual works are represented by capital letters; the volume of *Sam-*

lede Vaerker in which the work is contained is indicated by roman numerals.

The main translator of Kierkegaard's works into English is Walter Lowrie. I refer to his translation by LO and the number of the page, after the reference to the Danish edition. Examples: PV XIII 604 LO 76. The same principle applies where other English translations are cited.

We gratefully acknowledge our debt to the following publishers for quotations from Kierkegaard's works: Oxford University Press for excerpts from *The Journals, The Point of View for My Work as an Author, Training in Christianity, Christian Discourses,* and *The Present Age;* Princeton University Press for excerpts from *Kierkegaard's Attack upon "Christendom," Either/Or, Stages on Life's Way, Fear and Trembling, For Self-Examination, Sickness unto Death, The Works of Love, On Authority and Revelation: The Book on Adler,* and *The Concept of Dread;* Augsburg Publishing House for quotation from *Edifying Discourses.*

LIST OF KIERKEGAARD'S WORKS
(With Abbreviations of the Titles)

Kierkegaard As Theologian

I

THE ASCENT TO
THE RELIGIOUS LEVEL

1. *Kierkegaard's Family Background and Education*

KIERKEGAARD HIMSELF STATES that his life began in "1813, in that mad year when so many other mad bank-notes were put into circulation . . . and sometimes bank-notes of that kind are the misfortune of a whole family" (V A³) (477).

His father, Mikael Pedersen Kierkegaard, had been a shepherd lad on the barren Jutland moors until suddenly, at the age of twelve, he was called to Copenhagen to help in his uncle's flourishing haberdashery business. A few years later he took over the enterprise and managed it with such success that in less than twenty years he was able to sell the business and retire as a wealthy man. Just prior to his retirement his wife had died, leaving him no children. A year after her death he married his housekeeper, who gave birth to Mikael's first child five months after the wedding. Six children were to follow. Last of these was Soren Aabye: his father was fifty-six and his mother forty-five at the time.

3

Despite the material comfort a somber atmosphere prevailed in the household. Old Mikael was given to brooding as if a sinister event of his past life weighed heavily upon him. His melancholy reached a climax when, during a two-year period, his wife and all but two of his seven children died. From this time on he devoted himself to the religious education of his youngest son. His ideas of sin and penance had such an effect on the child that even as an adult Soren could not think of these years without a shudder.

By isolating his son from the world the elderly man tried to preserve him from evil, about which he himself seemed so profoundly shaken. Kierkegaard revered his father highly, but at the same time he developed an unconscious desire to cast off the latter's yoke. This ambivalent state of mind was to affect profoundly his life and work.

The diary clearly reveals the impact which the father's teaching had on Kierkegaard:

It is terrifying when a man's consciousness from his early childhood has been under a pressure which no elasticity of the soul, no energy of freedom, will ever be able to overcome. Mental suffering in life may press down upon consciousness, but when it appears at a more mature age, there is no time for it to establish itself in one's nature. It is only an historical moment, not something which weighs, as it were, on consciousness. Whoever bears this pressure within him, from his youth, is like a child, that has been removed with forceps from his mother's body and preserves, all through his life, the memory of his mother's pain (IV A 60) (420).[1]

Is the basis of the father's strong influence to be found only

[1] Other texts can be found in *The Point of View for My Work as an Author* (PV XIII 604 LO 76), and at the end of *Either/Or* where he sounds a warning note against an over-strict religious education of children, which, he says, causes them an anxiety that was unknown under heathenism.

in his religious education, or was there also, as some psychologists have maintained, an initial trauma in which his mother's role was even more important?[2] According to the latter view, Kierkegaard, as a result of an unconscious desire to possess his mother, constructed a frightening father-image which he gradually identified with his religious conscience.

Whatever one thinks of this hypothesis, it is certain that the influences of Kierkegaard's childhood were responsible for the tensions in his personality. The wish to surrender to the spontaneous inclination of his nature, coupled with the constant dread of yielding to such a wish, was to lead him to the most complicated forms of self-torture. Kierkegaard was never able to harmonize his instincts with what he considered his "better self." Flesh for him stood in constant opposition to spirit: each strove for domination—the one covertly and in secret, the other openly.

His great work, *Either/Or,* reveals a tense and intricate eroticism which reappears in some of his later works (e.g., *Stages on Life's Way*) and especially in the intimacy of his diary. On the other hand, his personality seems to have been centered exclusively on the spiritual element. He tended to transform everything into a principle and an idea, even, and particularly, his erotic life.[3]

The split in his personality was accentuated by the weakness of a body not built to accommodate an audacious spirit such as his own. Kierkegaard felt that he was almost completely lacking in what physically characterizes a normal man. The "animal" element was wanting in his personality (X³ A 115), (1105), or, as he put it, "My trouble is that I do

---

[2] See, for example, the study of H. Lowtzky, *Kierkegaard* (Vienna, 1935), and the more penetrating article of P. Esser, "Le développement et l'évolution de Kierkegaard," *Nederlandsch Tijdschrift voor Psychologie* (1936), p. 150.

[3] See, e.g., I A 476 (928).

not have enough body" (IX A 74). He possessed all the spiritual resources for work, but lacked the physical capability to
relax (VIII A 200). The secret suffering to which he constantly referred as "the thorn in the flesh" had undoubtedly
some relation to his body, even if it was, as I believe, basically
a psychological problem.[4]

The ambivalence in Kierkegaard's personality also explains
his ironical attitude. From his early boyhood he took a morbid delight in presenting himself in a frivolous light and in
hiding his serious, melancholy nature.[5] His own life is a
perfect illustration of what the diary (VI A 38 (516), X[1] A
186), and the *Postscript* (PS VII 492 LO 448) describe as
irony: to assume an outward attitude as different as possible
from one's internal state in order to intensify the opposition
between the absolute stature of the self and the numerous
trivia of social intercourse in which it has to express itself.
Irony consists in the conscious acceptance of the contradiction between one's infinite interiority and its deficient outward realization. By means of reflection the ironical person
interiorizes and dominates the opposition between his high
ethical ideals and the triviality of everyday life. He does not
eliminate the conflict but makes it conscious and takes an almost morbid delight in it. By this too self-conscious attitude, however, he becomes a spectator of himself and makes

---

[4] PV XIII 612 LO 82. Many a commentator has attempted to discover
in just what this suffering consisted. Some years ago a Danish scholar,
R. Magnussen, caused a sensation by theorizing that Kierkegaard had
been a hunchback. On the basis of this hypothesis he interpreted his
entire life. The fact is that Kierkegaard walked with his shoulders
hunched forward, and after his death his relatives emphasized his boyhood fall from a tree, an accident from which he never completely
recovered. Moreover, to judge from the vague hospital reports, he seems
to have died of a disease of the spinal marrow. But he was never a hunchback! This is obvious enough from the caricatures that the satirical
Copenhagen weekly, *The Corsair,* published of him.

[5] See I A 161 (53); also II A 132 (151) and II A 662.

spontaneous surrender impossible.[6] Irony, therefore, is not a mere cultural phenomenon but a necessary determination of the unhappy consciousness. It is not accidental that Kierke- gaard wrote his Magister's thesis on this subject and that it appears, at least implicitly, in most of his works.

Another aspect of Kierkegaard's psychological ambiguity is his anxiety. It is certainly remarkable that anxiety is, if not the subject, at least the main theme of three of his best works: *Fear and Trembling, The Concept of Dread,* and *Sickness unto Death.* The same state of mind is expressed even more strongly in his autobiographical *Quidam's Diary* from *Stages on Life's Way.*[7]

Modern psychology has explained the meaning of anxiety in the ambivalent personality as an alarm-signal indicating that there is a danger of psychic conflict between the ego and its instinctive impulses.[8] This interpretation agrees with the remarkable analysis which Kierkegaard, relying on his private experience, has left us in *The Concept of Dread.*

In contrast with fear, which is always fear *of something,* anxiety refers only to the indefinite possibilities of one's own freedom. Freedom involves a certain danger because in every important choice man's whole personality is at stake. At the same time, the risk of freedom is attractive, for it opens a world of possibilities in which man may realize himself. This vague awareness of danger combined with a feeling of at- traction—the "sympathetic antipathy and antipathetic sym-

[6] This clearly appears in the following entry concerning frustrated love: "Not to be able to possess the beloved is not irony. But to be able to possess her all too easily, so that she herself begs and prays to belong to one, and then not to be able to get her: that is irony" (VIII A 517) (727).

[7] In his personal diary he notes on May 12, 1839: "The whole of existence frightens me, from the smallest fly to the mystery of the in- carnation; everything is unintelligible to me, most of all myself" (II A 420) (275).

[8] Juliette Boutonier, *L'angoisse* (Paris, 1949).

pathy" which man experiences before his own possibilities—
is anxiety (IV A 346). However, to cause real anxiety, the
alarming extent of freedom must first appear to consciousness
as dangerously concrete. The sudden realization of a religious
or moral disproportion, or the real possibility of one, suffices
to awaken the latent anxiety. In Kierkegaard's case this occurred very vehemently in the crisis of his early manhood.

What was the terrible incident which the diary of 1839 (II
A 805) (243) describes as "the great earthquake"?[9] Did old
Mikael disclose to his son the dreadful mystery of his own
life? Or did Soren himself discover that his father, the column
against which he leaned for religious and moral support, was
a sinful man? The myth of David and Solomon (in *Quidam's
Diary*), which is certainly related to what happened at that
time, seems to confirm the latter supposition.

Solomon lived happily with the prophet Nathan. The father's
strength and the father's achievement did not inspire him to
deeds of valor, for in fact no occasion was left for that, but it

[9] On a loose page of his journal, written in 1839, we read the following mysterious words: "Then it was that the great earthquake occurred,
the terrible revolution which suddenly forced upon me a new and
infallible law of interpretation of all the facts. Then I suspected that my
father's great age was not a divine blessing but rather a curse; that
the outstanding intellectual gifts of our family were only given to us
in order that we should rend each other to pieces: then I felt the
stillness of death grow around me when I saw my father, an unhappy
man who was to outlive us all, a cross on the tomb of all his hopes.
There must be a guilt upon the whole family, the punishment of God
must be on it; it was to disappear, wiped out by the powerful hand of
God, obliterated like an unsuccessful attempt, and only at times did I
find a little alleviation in the thought that my father had been allotted
the heavy task of calming us with the consolation of religion, of minister-
ing to us so that a better world should be open to us even though we
lost everything in this world, even though we were overtaken by the
punishment which the Jews always called down upon their enemies:
that all recollection of us should be utterly wiped out, that we should
no longer be found" (II A 805) (243).

inspired him to admiration, and admiration made him a poet. But if the poet was almost jealous of his hero, the son was blissful in his devotion to the father.

Then the son one day made a visit to his royal father. In the night he awoke at hearing movement where the father slept. Horror seizes him, he fears it is a villain who would murder David. He steals nearer—he beholds David with a crushed and contrite heart, he hears a cry of despair from the soul of the penitent.

Faint at the sight he returns to his couch, he falls asleep but he does not rest, he dreams that David is an ungodly man, rejected by God, that the royal majesty is the sign of God's wrath upon him, that he must wear the purple as a punishment, that he is condemned to rule, condemned to hear the people's benediction, whereas the Lord's righteousness secretly and hiddenly pronounces judgment upon the guilty one; and the dream suggests the surmise that God is not the God of the pious but of the ungodly, and that one must be an ungodly man to be God's elect—and the horror of the dream is this contradiction (SL VI 265-266 LO 236-237).

This myth tells us, better than any direct communication could, the impact of what occurred between father and son. Perhaps an entry in the diary from 1844 can throw more light on the external circumstances of the event:

A relationship between father and son, where the son secretly discovers everything after, and yet dares not acknowledge it. The father is a respectable man, severe and God-fearing, only once in a state of intoxication he lets drop a few words which hint at the worst. Otherwise, the son does not discover what it is and never dares ask his father or others (V A 103) (503).

At another place in his diary Kierkegaard sketches, as a pure possibility, the case of a man who as a boy had had a difficult life and who one day, when suffering acutely from

hunger and cold, had cursed God on a lonely hill. The man
could never forget his act, not even when he was eighty-two
years old (VII A 5) (556). When, after Kierkegaard's death,
the first publisher of the journals showed this passage to
Kierkegaard's brother Peter, he exclaimed, "This is the story
of our father and ourselves." For all this, it is still not certain
that it was the discovery of this sin which led to the "earthquake." Soren might have suspected something about
Mikael's relations with his housekeeper, which had forced
him to marry her. Some think that perhaps other debauches
had preceded his rather late first marriage. Concerning all
this we are left in uncertainty; Kierkegaard suggested the secret of his life without actually revealing it. Only one thing is
sure: suddenly he saw that the life of his father, whom he
had enshrined as a saint, was in disharmony with God.

The reaction following this discovery was terrible. A period
of complete upheaval began; everything that had been holy
for Kierkegaard collapsed. He had lost all religious and moral
orientation. Regularly he came home drunk, and he continuously hovered on the verge of insanity. Faith itself became a large question mark, although he never abandoned
it. The inevitable moral fall finally took place in the spring
of 1836; it was to leave its stamp on his whole future life.
The diary makes no mention of it in that year, except for the
following mysterious note, dated October 8:

The extraordinary way in which something long forgotten suddenly bursts into consciousness is really quite remarkable; for
example, the recollection of something wrong, of which one was
hardly conscious at the moment of acting—lightning announc-
ing a violent storm (I A 254) (76) (cf. also CD IV 437 LO 114).

All indications are that this was the experience which
Kierkegaard described years later in his story of the insane
man of Christianshavn. Somewhere in Copenhagen there

was a young man employed in his parents' business. He lived completely apart from the world, behaved well, and was happy. But one day there came over him a vague suspicion that something was lacking in his life, that he had missed something. And indeed he had missed something: he had forgotten to be young and to give his heart joy in the days of his youth. So he became acquainted with some young people. One evening they went out together and visited "one of those places where one gives money for a woman's despicableness" (SL VI 298 LO 264). The intoxication left only a hazy recollection of what had occurred, but gradually the possibility that he had begotten a child drove him insane.

Kierkegaard himself has described the moral decline which reached a climax at this period as a result of the consciousness "that the one man he revered for his power and strength had wavered" (IV A 107) (444).

In the Antigone theme he first suggested the anxiety aroused by the discovery of his father's sin. Dim suspicions gradually lead Oedipus' daughter to the horrible secret of her father's incest "until certainty, with a single blow, casts her into the arms of anxiety" (EO I 152 LO 125). Later in 1843 (the same year as the above entry), he returned to this motif in an attempt to explain *guilt* through anxiety. But for this purpose the innocent figure of Antigone was not suitable. He then invented the myth of Solomon (IV A 114), which ultimately led to the passage of the *Stages* that we quoted above.

Far from liberating him from his father's influence, the earthquake gave Kierkegaard a terrible feeling of guilt. The subconscious image of his father remained untarnished; the guilt became his own. Unconsciously he identified himself with his father's guilt, and this feeling of guilt brought him, paradoxically enough, to sin. Guilt already lay upon him; the sin needed only to be committed.

In the myth of David and Urias, Kierkegaard reflects on this feeling of *guilt before sin*. He relates how David decided to effect Urias' death in order to marry his wife, Bathsheba. The messenger has already departed with David's order, and David retires. But he finds no sleep; remorse fills him with terror at his decision. At that moment of repentance he realizes that the murder might still be averted, and he summons another messenger to send a countermanding order. Now David is abiding the result, for five long days. What are five days? It seems an insignificant time, but five days of repentance for a crime which has not even been committed might well turn a man's hair gray. For there is a great difference between having decided to be a murderer and being one (SL VI 473 LO 408).

He similarly interprets Hamlet's hesitations, after he had conceived the plan of killing his stepfather, as a feeling of guilt before the sin (SL VI 477 LO 410). This feeling causes remorse, mingled with anxiety, which can drive a man almost unwillingly to sin:

The dialectic form of repentance is this: he cannot get to the point of repenting because it is as though it were still undetermined what he is to repent of; and he cannot find repose in repentance, because it is as though he ought constantly to be doing something, undoing what was done if that were possible (SL VI 474 LO 408).

It is in the feeling of guilt that the ambiguity of Kierkegaard's personality becomes most evident. Typical is the title of his most intimate writing: *Quidam's Diary: Guilty—Not Guilty*. His guilt is primarily a feeling of remorse before God, but it also implies guilt in his relation to his father. How closely the two are connected, appears in a little note, written on his twenty-fifth birthday, when he reconciled himself with his father after several years of estrangement:

How I thank you, Father in Heaven, that you have preserved my earthly father here upon earth for a time such as this when I so greatly need him, a father who, as I hope, will with your help have greater joy in being my father a second time than he had the first time in being (II A 231) (210).

Shortly after the reconciliation Mikael Pedersen died. Years later Kierkegaard was to say that this shock put a definite end to the dissolute period of his life (VIII A 650) (754). Fear of guilt had given way to accomplished guilt.

His former fiancée, Regine Olsen, once revealed that, during their engagement, Soren's conversations constantly returned to one subject: he had been a bad son to his father, and had not shown him enough affection. Kierkegaard's abnormal relation to his father was probably the main obstacle which prevented him from marrying her.

2. The Engagement

Here we come to the second relationship which had a marked influence on Kierkegaard's life. Looking back over his career, he was to declare that his entire creative activity owed its origin to one fact: his engagement with Regine Olsen.

The story is a simple one. On September 10, 1840, Kierkegaard betrothed himself to a seventeen-year-old girl from Copenhagen, and one year later, after much hesitation, he returned her ring. In this commonplace series of events lies the drama of his life, because he knew that he had broken her heart and made himself unhappy forever. Why did he, consciously and voluntarily, elect this suffering? Regine Olsen was to say in her declining years that this mystery between them had never been clarified. However, Kierkegaard's personal Journal and *Quidam's Diary* tell us enough about it to understand how it could take place.

That Kierkegaard broke his engagement was mainly due to inhibitions he had acquired in childhood. The catastrophic implications of a stringent religious and moral education in which the father had tried to preserve his son from his own failures now became effective. Kierkegaard himself realized remarkably well the true cause of his misery:

If a child were told that it was a sin to break its leg, what terror it would live in, and probably break it often, thinking that it was a sin even to have been in danger of breaking it. Suppose it were impossible for him to overcome that childhood's impression. Then out of love for his parents and in order that their blunder should not end terribly in his own ruin, he would endure it as long as possible. A horse that is harnessed to too great a load pulls with all its might and falls down.

And sometimes people are led astray as to what sin is, and the cause is perhaps some well-meaning person. For example a man who has been very dissolute, in order to frighten his son from anything of the same kind, might explain that sexual desire was in itself sinful—forgetting that there was a difference between himself and the child—that the child was innocent and would therefore of necessity misunderstand him. The unhappy man, who even as a child was harnessed to pull and toil through life! (VI A 105) (539).

Kierkegaard was never able to come to terms with sex. Carnal intercourse always remained sinful in his eyes. His entire education led him to see in women only an object of sinful lust. Nevertheless, owing perhaps to the mother-image, he felt himself drawn to woman as to an ideal of pure innocence which might liberate his highest spiritual possibilities. But he was never able to reconcile these two aspects. In *Either/Or* and *Stages on Life's Way* he alternately emphasizes, under different pseudonyms, woman as object of sensual desire and woman as redemption. He shocked his contemporaries by the sensuous eroticism of *The Diary of the Seducer* (from *Either/Or*) and went even further in *In Vino Veritas* (from the *Stages*). But the same books also contain two fragments on the spiritual meaning of marriage which are among the most sublime passages ever written on this subject. Kierkegaard always maintained that neither standpoint was his own: they depict two aspects of his personality which he could not reconcile. Gradually the lust aspect of woman seems to gain prominence, so that she becomes the decisive element in the choice between the "aesthetic" life (governed by lust) and the religious (in which lust is entirely abandoned). Continence then becomes the only appropriate attitude for the Christian and he abandons the classic Protestant ideal of marriage. In *The Instant* (1855) his attacks on marriage reach an extreme which has probably never been equalled by any religious writer:

I am unable to comprehend how it can occur to any man to unite being a Christian with being married. Note that with this I am not thinking of the case of a man who was already married and had a family, and then at that age became a Christian; no, I mean to say, how one who is unmarried and says he has become a Christian, how it would occur to him to marry (IN XIV 316 LO 213).

Kierkegaard's attitude toward woman was entirely determined by anxiety: she attracted him as an ideal of purity and at the same time repelled him as a threat to his spiritual existence. The stronger the dread, the greater the fascination. As a result, woman played an unusually important role in his life. But anxiety always prevented him from decisively giving himself to any particular woman.

This reservation in love appears clearly in his personal notes and in *Quidam's Diary*. The early stage of infatuation,

with its alternation of reserve and surrender, was all that
Kierkegaard seemed able to accept. After having broken
with Regine, he had to admit to himself that he had never
in earnest wanted to marry her (III A 166) (383).

Not less symptomatic of Kierkegaard's ambivalent attitude[10] is the fact that after the engagement had ended he
tried in every possible way to maintain his relationship with
Regine. A simple nod from her during Evensong of Easter
Sunday opened a world of possibilities for him: he seriously
contemplated renewing the affair. Despite the feeling of
relief, he found it painful that Regine was engaged to her
former friend, Frederik Schlegel. After her marriage he attempted a reconciliation with her father, but was sent away
(IX A 262) (815). Later, he asked in a letter Schlegel's permission to resume contact with his wife, but, understandably
enough, was turned down. It was only then that Kierkegaard
realized that the separation was irrevocable. However, his last
link with Regine was not severed until a few months before
his death. On the eve of her departure for the Danish West
Indies, Regine managed to meet him on the street and
whispered, "God bless you, may everything go according to
your wishes!" Kierkegaard was startled and could only wave
good-bye. It almost looks as if his erotic drive could find
release only in torturing himself and his partner in love.

The self-destructive tendency which appeared in his eroticism also showed itself in his continuous obsession with death.
After discovering his father's guilt, Kierkegaard was certain

---

[10] E.g. II A 273 (227). Professor G. Van der Leeuw thus summarizes the
ambivalence in Kierkegaard's erotic relations: "He is at once lover and
contemplator of his love. He cannot decide to be a man and not a
woman. He is afraid of the consequences of having children; woman is
the maiden and should not become anything else. Thus he prefers vague
eroticism to love, contemplation at a distance to action." "De Psychologie van Kierkegaard," *Algemeen Nederlandsch Tijdschrift voor
Wijsbegeerte en Psychologie,* II (1934), p. 23.

that he would die before his twenty-fifth birthday; hence, the title of his first literary effort published shortly after that date: *From the Papers of One Still Living*. The idea returned in 1848: Kierkegaard believed that his task was accomplished and that he was about to die. Thereupon he composed *The Point of View for My Work as an Author*. The same attitude is revealed in a sketch which he included, quite out of any context, in his diary: A melancholy individual kills himself without any motive or premeditation, "just as one stoops and plucks a flower." Death here is "potentialized voluptuousness" (X¹ A 642) (952).

In his relationship with Regine the idea of death continually appeared. The fulfillment of his love would be possible only in death.

My one consolation is that I could lie down and die and then in the hour of my death admit to the love which as long as I live I dare not do, and which makes me equally happy and unhappy (III A 90) (349).

That Kierkegaard also considered suicide is certain from the following notation in which he conceives the idea of returning to Regine and then perishing by his own hand:

And indeed if I did not abhor suicide, did I not feel that all such virtues were but shining vices, then I should turn back to her—in order then to end my life, a plan which unfortunately has been all too long in my mind and which makes the separation from her doubly hard for me. For who loves like a dying man, and that is really how I have always thought of it each time I have devoted myself to her, and to live with her in the peaceful and trusting sense of the word never occurred to me (III A 159) (377).

But he realized that his death would only bring a new calamity upon her: she would feel guilty. Therefore he

wanted to destroy himself in her eyes so completely that she
could only hate him. Kierkegaard compared his behavior
with that of a mother who blackens her breast to wean her
child (FT III 74 LO 12). He presented to Regine his entire
relationship with her as if he had been only a deceiver who
had wished to seduce her: "Humanly speaking, this was the
only way to save her and to give her soul vitality" (III A 166)
(383).

In their last conversation his answer to her question
whether he ever intended to marry sounds sadistic:

"Yes, perhaps in ten years time when I have sown my wild oats;
then I shall need some young blood to rejuvenate me" (VIII A
108) (657).

Only by destroying himself and his companion does Kierkegaard feel able to fulfill his love.

Just as he punished Regine in himself, he could only love
her in *himself:* his whole affective life was wrapped up in
his own person. Kierkegaard had imprisoned himself in
himself, lest he lose himself in the other, whereas only such
surrender would have saved him. As it was, he always remained suspended between the deeply felt need for spontaneous communication with others and the impossibility of
satisfying this need. Characteristic of this narcissism is what
he wrote in his diary in 1849:

This fault I also have that I constantly accompany myself poet-
ically and now require of myself almost in desperation that I shall
act so as to be in character (X^1 A 513) (937).[11]

He saw his love for Regine as if it were a grace given by
him, to which she owed all her spiritual riches.

[11] P. Mesnard has made a good analysis of Kierkegaard's narcissism
in his relations with Regine, in *Le vrai visage de Kierkegaard* (Paris,
1948), p. 274.

... and I loved her dearly, she was as light as a bird, as daring as a thought; I let her rise higher and higher, I stretched out my hand and she settled on it and beat her wings and called down to me: It is wonderful here; she forgot, she did not know that it was I who made her light, I who gave her daring in thought; faith in me which made her walk upon the waters, and I swore allegiance to her and she accepted my homage (III A 133) (363).

His intimacy with himself incapacitated him for close friendships:

Like a solitary fir tree, egotistically constricted and towering loftily, I stand without casting a shadow, and only the wood pigeon makes its nest in my branches (II A 617).

Typical in this connection was his relationship with Rasmus Nielsen. After years of hostility the young philosophy professor greeted Kierkegaard on the street. The latter responded, and so they began an acquaintance in which the teacher eventually became the pupil. During Nielsen's frequent visits Kierkegaard gave him a direct interpretation of his works. We are ill-impressed when, after this intimate relation, we find Kierkegaard remarking that he used this one friend only for his own development (X^1 A 280) (905). It is even less to his credit that he became highly suspicious of Nielsen's motives. When the latter's *magnum opus* was published, and Kierkegaard's name had received no mention in it, he accused Nielsen of having been merely friendly and flattering in his personal relations in order tacitly to deny him as an author. He drew a comparison with Socrates and Plato, but with the difference that this Plato forgot to mention to whom he owed his ideas (X^3 A 146) (1108).

All this leaves us with the impression that Kierkegaard was psychologically immature, a person concerned only with himself. Some pages of the diary confirm this impression

with their almost repulsive vanity and self-dramatization.[12]
This was especially shown after the attacks of the satirical
Copenhagen weekly, *The Corsair.* Printed under the direction of the able M. A. Goldschmidt, and with the secret
collaboration of the litterateur, P. L. Moller, this unscrupu-
lous little sheet had, during the year 1845, mentioned Kierkegaard's work with approval. The latter, however, was not
pleased with this honor: he did not want to be in favor with
people who disparaged all that was good in Denmark.
Eulogies from this quarter could only lead to misunderstanding of his work. At about the same time Moller contributed
an article in his own name to *Gea, Esthetic Annals for 1846;*
this review praised *Either/Or* highly, but contained nothing
but adverse criticism for the *Stages.* Kierkegaard was worried
that people might interpret his aesthetic writings apart from
their religious context. Even before the publication of the
Annals he wrote a stinging essay, under the pseudonym
Frater Taciturnus, which concluded with the unmasking of
Moller and expressed the wish that his own name might appear as soon as possible in *The Corsair,* "because it is really
hard for a poor author to be the only one in Danish literature
who is not detracted. . . . And yet I have appeared there
already, because *ubi spiritus ibi ecclesia, ubi* P. L. Moller
ibi The Corsair" (VII[1] B 1).

Kierkegaard had to wait less than a week to receive what
he had requested. On January 2 there appeared an article
entitled, "How the Wandering Philosopher Discovered the
Real Author of *The Corsair.*" The attacks immediately became very personal. In the issue of January 9 there was a

---

[12] "Really, what country would not consider itself fortunate to have
an author like me, especially a country as small as Denmark, which will
certainly never have my equal again?" (IX A 120). "My literary activity,
. . . in rivalling one work of which not a single one of my contemporaries
could succeed, not to speak of it as a whole—this literary activity is
regarded as a kind of amateurism, like going fishing" (IX A 288).

piece about Kierkegaard's strange mode of dress. The latter wrote a final sharp reply in *The Fatherland*. After that the dam burst: a stream of irony and coarse wit flooded over Kierkegaard, so that he could not even appear on the street without being stared at or even derided by everyone. By October of the same year the attack was to end with the discontinuance of *The Corsair*. But the malice had done its damage, and in these few months Kierkegaard had become the laughingstock of Copenhagen, which he would remain until the end of the century. His person became a butt of student parodies. How deeply this attack affected him appears in the hundreds of pages that he devoted to it in the diary.

Yet Kierkegaard seemed to forget that it was he who had touched off the explosion. And it is doubtful whether his sole motive had been to take forceful action, in the name of all right-minded people, against the unethical mudslinging of *The Corsair*. It seems to us that here again, seeking to become the center of attention, Kierkegaard wanted to be the only man who was not afraid of *The Corsair*. A latent desire for derision and self-pity might have played an even greater part in his attitude.[13]

His complaints, however justified, provide us with an idea

---

[13] That these feelings were not strange to Kierkegaard appears from hundreds of diary entries, mostly written in the years 1848-1849, in the style of this one: "And even though Denmark were willing to do so, it is very questionable whether Denmark could make good the wrong it has done me. That I am an author in whom Denmark will undoubtedly take pride, is certain; that, qua author, I have lived, to all intents and purposes, at my own expense and without assistance from government or people, have borne a continuous literary production without the smallest literary support from a periodical because I saw how small the country was: and then to have had such treatment, my biggest work not even reviewed—the machinery of the whole plan hardly suspected: and then its author marked out by all that is vulgar and known to every shoemaker's boy who in the name of "public opinion" insults him on the street (for the press after all is public opinion) : no, no Denmark has condemned itself" (IX A 169) (794).

of what Kierkegaard's contemporaries meant by his morbid "irritability."[14] He considered himself a martyr with a task "more difficult than anyone, anyone in Christendom has ever had imposed upon him" (X¹ A 315). Society never accepted him because he always withdrew into himself and never learned the intricate but usually spontaneous game of give-and-take. The responsibility was therefore as much Kierkegaard's as his contemporaries', and the campaign of *The Corsair* only served to accentuate this situation.

This incapacity to be spontaneous, or, as he himself called it, "immediate," could not but make his engagement to a young and lively girl a real torture. He felt that he was involved in a situation that he could not master, and one which he did not wish to master, either. Kierkegaard more than others was sensitive to the charm of Regine's spontaneous beauty, but he also realized that, to respond to it, he would have to abandon the best of himself; he was able to live only in a reflective dimension. A page from the pseudonymous account of his own love, *Guilty—Not Guilty,* depicts this ambivalent attitude strikingly.

I cannot keep my soul fixed upon the immediacy of love. I see indeed that she is charming, to my eyes indescribably charming. . . . But this childlike happiness, this lightness in the world which I cannot understand and with which I cannot sympathize deeply and essentially (because my sympathy with it is through the medium of sadness, which precisely manifests the contradiction) —and my heroic struggle, my courage (to mention something good on my side), my lightness in dancing over abysses, of which she can have no conception and with which she can sympathize only unessentially, as with a dreadful tale one reads without being

[14] Thus the Swedish journalist Frederika Bremer in her *Life in the North* (Stockholm, 1849), pp. 53-55, and Goldschmidt—who is not a very objective witness however—in his *Nord og Syd* (1855), p. 200.

able to think of it as real—what will come of this? So I have chosen
the religious (SL VI 234-235 LO 210-211).

It is not easy to estimate the worth of the religiousness into
which his relationship with Regine led him. At first sight
his decision to abandon her seems to have been inspired by a
reflectivity which has nothing to do with religion. What right
has he to consider his renunciation of the "immediate" as
religious? Kierkegaard's assertion seems to imply that religion
must necessarily be reflective and dialectical.[15] Authentic
religion, according to him, appears only at the end of reflection, as a spiritual *return upon oneself,* an interiorization
of consciousness. Whether, and to what extent, this is really
the case will be discussed in the subsequent chapters. At this
point we are only attempting to discover how much Kierkegaard's incapacity to live spontaneously determined his religious categories.

3. *The Religious Meaning of*
Kierkegaard's Psychology

At first sight Kierkegaard's religious attitude appears as a
mere reflection of his relation to his father. Central is the
idea of God's fatherhood, which he consistently relates to its
origin, his earthly father (IX A 106) (578), (X[3] A 792) (1181),
(III A 73) (335). The ambivalent relationship with his father
was transferred to a religious plane.

The dread with which my father filled my soul, his own frightful melancholy, and all the things in this connection which I do

---

[15] What Kierkegaard understands by *dialectical* and *reflective* will become clearer in the following chapter. For our present purposes it
suffices to know that he opposes it to the spontaneous, the immediate.

not even note down. I felt a dread of Christianity and yet felt myself so strongly drawn towards it (IX A 411) (841).

Kierkegaard's attitude toward Christianity oscillated constantly between attraction and aversion. This aversion was at the basis of the ferocious attack of his last years against the Danish Church.[16] In his youth it manifested itself in a vague discomfiture concerning orthodoxy. In 1835, in a letter to his brother-in-law, Peter W. Lund, he wrote about the tremendous attraction he felt toward theology, but he also openly admitted the great difficulties which seemed to him inherent in Christian doctrine.

In Christianity itself the contradictions are so great that, to say the least, they prevent a clear view. As you know I grew up so to speak in orthodoxy; but as soon as I began to think for myself the tremendous colossus began to totter (I A 72) (16).

In another place he speaks of "the strange, oppressive atmosphere" in Christianity which is stifling and which creates a most dangerous climate (I A 99) (32). That these were not temptations of an isolated moment is apparent from *Quidam's Diary*, published ten years later, in which the same doubts reappear (SL VI 273 LO 242-243).

Kierkegaard's aversion to Christianity was so pronounced during one period that we might wonder whether he did not lose his faith. This interpretation, however, seems to be refuted by his autobiographical work, *The Point of View for My Work as an Author*, in which he explicitly denies ever having been abandoned, even for an instant, by faith (PV XIII 604 LO 76-77). Faith made him unhappy as would an

---

[16] It is all too obvious that Kierkegaard himself was not conscious of those hidden motives: consciously he acted only in the name of Christianity.

unhappy love, which, nevertheless, one would not be willing to lose.

So I loved Christianity in a way: to me it was venerable—it had, to be sure, humanly speaking, rendered me exceedingly unhappy. This corresponds to my relationship with my father, the person whom I loved most deeply. And what is the meaning of this? The point precisely is that he made me unhappy—but out of love. His error did not consist in lack of love, but in mistaking a child for an old man. To love him who makes one happy, is to a reflective mind an inadequate definition of what love is; to love him who made one unhappy out of malice, is virtue; but to love him who out of love, though by a misunderstanding yet out of love, made one unhappy—that is the formula never yet enunciated, so far as I know, but nevertheless the normal formula in reflection for what it is to love (PV XIII 605 LO 77).

The religious influence of his father became most obvious in Kierkegaard's relations with Bishop Mynster. When still a parish curate, Mynster frequently used to visit the Kierkegaard home; Mikael Pedersen considered him both a spiritual director and a friend. When he became Bishop of Sealand, this sympathetic bond grew into a deep veneration. Young Soren was nurtured with Mynster's spiritual food, and gradually the old bishop came to exercise the same spiritual fatherhood over him that he once did over his father. Little by little Mynster came to stand in the same light of ambivalent piety in which Kierkegaard viewed everything that concerned his father. Kierkegaard called on him regularly, and during his engagement he tried for a time to raise Regine to his own religious level by now and then reading one of Mynster's sermons to her. Moreover, immediately upon publication of each of his books, Kierkegaard would faithfully request the Bishop's judgment.

But here also, in time, an unconscious desire to shake off the yoke began to manifest itself. Mynster to him personified the entire dead weight of the "established order" which lay upon Christianity. The Bishop was too conservative, too anxious to preserve his position, too much a civil servant. Besides, Kierkegaard never forgave him for not having lifted a finger in his support during the attack by *The Corsair*. Nevertheless, Kierkegaard felt himself committed to Mynster, for the latter represented the spiritual bond with his father. In a diary entry of 1848 he concluded a lengthy critique with these words:

And yet I like Bishop Mynster, my only desire is to do everything to increase his prestige; for I admired him, and humanly speaking I still do admire him. Every time that I can do something to help him, I think of my father, and I believe that that gives him pleasure (IX A 85).

It was in *Training in Christianity* that, after many near misses, there first occurred a real collision. In this book Kierkegaard vehemently denounced the sad condition of Christianity in Denmark and made some thinly veiled personal attacks on the bishop. In private, Mynster spoke in very sharp terms about the book. When, some time after publication, Kierkegaard called on Mynster to hear his opinion, the latter said that the first half of the book was an attack on Martensen—the Hegelian theology professor who would be his successor—and the second half an attack on himself. That seemed to end the subject and the two men took leave on good terms.

Perhaps it was partial revenge on the bishop's part that in his own next book he extolled the talents of Goldschmidt, the former editor-in-chief of *The Corsair*. At any rate, this time it was Kierkegaard's turn to feel hurt. Another meeting

followed, in which each defended his own position. Once
again a short conversation about Kierkegaard's father confirmed the reconciliation. But not for long, for both men
differed so utterly in their religious ideas that a final break
was inevitable. The memory of Mikael Pedersen, which held
them together now, would only turn Kierkegaard all the
more against the bishop. In Mynster he saw the religious
image of his father, which he respected but at the same time
abhorred. Mynster was almost the embodiment of Kierkegaard's own religious education. Many texts reveal the same
ambivalence of affection and aversion which Kierkegaard
felt for his father.

The relationship remained amicable until Mynster's death,
but all the while tension between them was developing.
Kierkegaard had thought that an eruption was inevitable,
but his father's memory always remained uppermost. No
sooner had Mynster died, however, than, with a vehemence
that suggested the violation of a corpse, all the aggression that
Kierkegaard had unconsciously harbored against his father
was set free. As long as old Mikael was alive, the son could
not but love him despite everything. So long as the old man
who represented his father's Christianity was alive, this same
relation had prevailed. But when death also removed the
living image of his father, Kierkegaard's aggression was finally
released.

He himself never realized what secret forces were at work
here: he was convinced that he acted only on doctrinal
grounds. He believed that he was no longer permitted to
spare anyone, that he must act exclusively according to his
principles. A month after Mynster's death he noted:

The situation is also changed as regards my melancholy devotion
to my father's priest; for it would be too much of a good thing
if I could not talk about him more freely even after his death,

however well I know that my old devotion to him and my esthetic admiration will always continue to be attractive to me (XI¹ A 1) (1296).

At the end of the same year, 1854, he published a famous article in which he severely criticized the late bishop's work and simultaneously launched a full-scale onslaught against the national Church. That Kierkegaard attacked the Church only in the name of the Gospel in no way contradicts what we have said previously concerning his ambivalent attitude, but rather confirms it. Because his attitude was two-sided, and he loved what he fought, he would always destroy with one hand what he supported with the other.[17]

In addition to the influence of his father, as we have noted, the second element which marked his religious development was his broken engagement. Kierkegaard himself described the effect of this unhappy love affair on his religious life in two little books, published simultaneously two years after his break with Regine: *The Repetition* and *Fear and Trembling*.[18]

In *The Repetition*, Kierkegaard inquired into the possibility of perpetuating a transitory reality while maintaining its immediacy. His experience with Regine had taught him that he was unable to achieve an immediate relationship: the "immediacy" is resolved into reflection, the sensuous is spiritualized into a memory. Already in *Either/Or* Kierkegaard had described the danger of transforming real life into poetic memory:

---

[17] From his own principles it will appear that no form of established Christianity will ever find favor in his eyes, and therefore, it is after all Christianity itself that he attacks in the name of Christianity.

[18] For a good commentary on both works from this particular angle, see R. Bespaloff, "Notes sur la Repetition," *Revue Philosophique de la France et de l'Etranger*, 117 (1934), pp. 335-63; "En marge de *Crainte et Tremblement* de Kierkegaard," *Ibid.*, 119 (1935), pp. 43-72.

There is nothing more dangerous to me than remembering. The moment I have remembered some life relationship, that moment it ceased to exist. People say that separation tends to revive love. Quite true, but it revives it in a purely poetic manner. . . . A remembered life relation has already passed into eternity, and has no more temporal interest (EO I 19 LO 26).

Kierkegaard's reflective attitude made impossible an *actual* union in love and compelled him to experience his relationship with Regine exclusively by remembrance. From the tragic tension caused by a desire to live at once reflectively and immediately arose the question of whether the reflectivity of memory could be endowed with the intensity of actual realization. He thought that Christianity offered the solution, for in it eternity, penetrating into time, removes the present of earthly existence from the condition of transitoriness. In God, the past—and human love as well—acquires eternal actuality. Consequently, the religious experience brings about a new immediacy which is no longer subject to the vicissitudes of the sensuous.

In this view religion is still subordinated to purely human interests and restricted to the role of perpetuating an unfulfilled sensuous love. However, on the same day as *The Repetition* Kierkegaard also published *Fear and Trembling*. These works, according to the intention of their author, must be taken as two complementary aspects of a single attitude toward life.

In *Fear and Trembling* Kierkegaard took up the example of the aging Abraham, ascending Mount Moriah at God's command to sacrifice his only son, yet still believing in God's promises for a numerous posterity. By his sacrifice Abraham abandoned earthly reality, but by his trust in the divine promises he was admitted to a new reality. So Abraham regained everything "by virtue of the absurd," that is, by faith against all reasonable expectations. Kierkegaard, too, had abandoned all his earthly desires, in the person of Regine, and had thereby reached religion's threshold. But, as he put it, he never became a knight of faith like Abraham, because he merely arrived at the point of renouncing the mundane, without ever fully achieving the new reality of faith. "Had I had faith," he wrote in his diary, "I should have remained with Regine" (IV A 107) (444).

I believe that this insight in *Fear and Trembling* opened the way for Kierkegaard to true religion. All that precedes it was so greatly deformed by his abnormal upbringing and warped psychology that it appears to be a disguised projection of subconscious drives rather than authentic religion. But what Kierkegaard discovered in *Fear and Trembling* was no longer a sublimation of subconscious urges but a *new reality*, which he experienced in sharp contrast with his own morbid attitude. Kierkegaard's flight from reality seems to have driven him to religion as an escape, but a deeper reflection on the religious ideal brought him back to reality. Religion itself had changed in the process: from an escape of reality it became an over-all acceptance of it on a higher level. Hence, I cannot agree with R. Bespaloff's judgment: "His incapability of loving human beings leaves a certain need for love, which concentrates itself on God without ever reaching Him."[19]

Psychic inhibitions caused him to break his engagement, but the religious resignation with which he accepted his impotence made it into a conscious sacrifice that eventually would disclose to him the full, genuine reality of man. In this respect his difficult life is not the closed circle of a neurotic person, but the ascent of a man to religion.

This does not mean that Kierkegaard became a "well-adjusted" person, but rather that his psychology, however

[19] "Notes sur la Repetition," *art. cit.,* p. 359.

one-sided and deformed, transcended its limitations through religion and came to grips with *reality*. Any interpretation of his work as merely the exceptionally brilliant projection of psychic abnormality is, therefore, wholly inadequate. Undoubtedly his unique approach to religion exposed him to one-sidedness in the description of its phenomena, and so limited his point of view. But this does not intrinsically affect the transpsychic character of the reality which he described. Kierkegaard's psychology did not create his religious philosophy, but was only the occasion, or, better, the necessary condition, for its discovery. Rather than serving as an explanation of his work, Kierkegaard's psychological constitution should be explained in the light of his writings, for it is essentially subordinated to the reality with which they are concerned.

In this respect I agree completely with E. Przywara:

The depth of Kierkegaard's psychology is not the depth psychology of psychoanalysis but the psychology of the "depths of God," "Christian psychology," as Haecker rightly calls it. Yes, according to this interpretation we ought to say: the Kierkegaard of psychoanalysis is the "prey" pursued by the "Divine Hunter" of "Christian psychology."[20]

Inheritance and education predestined Kierkegaard to a serious confrontation with religion, but they did not make him religious. His attitude, therefore, was ultimately the result of his own free decision and perhaps of another factor which Kierkegaard mentions: grace (VIII A 161) (673).[21]

[20] E. Przywara, *Das Geheimnis Kierkegaards* (Munich, 1929), p. 43.
[21] This argument is conclusive only if one accepts the possibility of an authentic religious consciousness. If, on the contrary, one interprets all the categories of religious consciousness as mere sublimations of lower psychic strivings, a strictly *religious* development is *a priori* excluded. No doubt, even the most authentic religiousness is in great part marked by subconscious psychic tendencies. But it seems to us that, in Kierke-

Whether Kierkegaard, in spite of his psychological inhibitions, ever reached the authentically religious is a question the reader may answer for himself at the end of this book. Here I can only point out how the transition from one level to another occurred, and what *function* his personal psychology fulfilled in this development. For surely in Kierkegaard's case it was functional, that is to say, subordinate to a whole that encompassed it.

It is impossible to draw a perfectly clear line between psychologically determined experience and what we have called the authentically religious. Freedom and determinism are not isolated realities. They always appear together. No act is absolutely free and only very few are completely determined. The same holds true for religion. No religious experience is entirely independent of the rest of our psychological life. I do not think that there is such a thing as pure religion. But to explain religious experience in terms of its codetermining factors is to miss the essence of the religious phenomenon itself. This would be the same as to explain a work of art by a case history of its author.

The autonomy of Kierkegaard's religion, which I am trying to establish, is not psychological, as if his whole personal religious life became authentic and free from one certain moment on. It is specifically religious *insofar* as it does escape from being *qualitatively determined* by nonreligious factors. Kierkegaard's individual psychology can no more be separated from his religion in an exposition of his dialectic than it could be in his personal life. This admixture also implies

---

gaard's case, religious consciousness so greatly transcends the determinations of the more instinctive aspects of the personality that it constitutes a new psychic phenomenon. By this transcendence, in my view, authentic religiousness is distinguished from the inauthentic. Needless to say, this "transcendence" is not the same as what is called the "transcendent" origin of religion: it is a psychic phenomenon, and as such, however autonomous in its own sphere, it is essentially immanent.

that a total acceptance of his religious dialectic will be impossible. In fact, such an assent would be contrary to his own intention; Kierkegaard's dialectic is the dialectic of his own life. His work was never meant to impose a system, but to arouse in us the same vital dialectic which led him to discover religious existence.

Kierkegaard himself realized full well the peculiarity and unwholesomeness of his personality; he also knew how to distinguish it from religion. But at the same time he felt that these psychological weaknesses acquired a new meaning from religion. The rupture with Regine had been inspired not by purely religious motives, but by psychic impotence. However, it led him to a deeper religious consciousness and thus earned a functional role in the whole of his vocation.

I do not maintain and have never maintained that I did not marry because it was supposed to be contrary to Christianity, as though my being unmarried were a form of Christian perfection. Oh, far from it, had I been a man, the danger for me would certainly have been another, to have given myself all too much to women, and I might possibly have become a seducer. But this much is certain, my greatest pleasure would have been to marry the girl to whom I was engaged; God knows how much I wanted to: but here again is my wretchedness. *And so I remained unmarried,* and so I had the opportunity of thinking over what Christianity really meant by praising the unmarried state (X^2 A 61) (970).

From this standpoint the tragic story of his engagement receives spiritual significance: it was here that Kierkegaard became conscious of himself as a "point of intensity" which was not to develop in existence (X^1 A 671). The same applies to his misguided education.

Kierkegaard regarded himself as an outcast, moved by a higher force (X^2 A 587). A good many texts in the diary

4444444444

elaborate on this in concrete detail. Without his strict "education," his literary talents and religious sentiment would never have made him more than a religious poet (X^1 A 11) (861). Suffering has driven him to God as his "only consolation and beatitude" (X^3 A 182). He compared himself to a ship which has sustained damage even from its launching; in the extreme effort to keep himself afloat, he has developed an eminently spiritual existence (VIII A 185). Without psychic suffering he would never have achieved a real spiritual life. For a person in good health the immediate takes priority at once, whereas the spiritual life betokens the death of the immediate (X^1 A 645) (954).

Oh the thorn in the flesh has broken me once and for all in a finite sense—but eternally speaking I only spring higher. Perhaps that is right (VIII A 158) (670).

The same interpretation holds true of his ill-treatment by the public as a result of the affair with *The Corsair*. Kierkegaard himself declared that after the *Postscript* he had decided to give up his literary career, but that the incident with *The Corsair* forced him to go on (X^2 A 586). This collision taught him the profound opposition between Christianity and *the world*, a fact which would otherwise have escaped his notice, concentrated as he was on the interior (X^1 A 676).

His psychological problems, however humiliating, became meaningful in the context of his whole religious destiny. Kierkegaard was perfectly well aware that it was not virtue on his part that prevented him from accepting an ecclesiastical appointment, but rather melancholy, which made him incapable of leading a normal human existence. But at the same time this attitude taught him why the preaching of Christian doctrine is so difficult to combine with a salaried position (X^2 A 61) (970).

He fully realized that the many worries which he himself had created were nothing more than self-torture, but he also knew that this terrible suffering had, with God's help, given him ethical *depth* (X¹ A 275). As he himself pointed out in the *Stages*, introversion and melancholy induce a crisis of despair in which man becomes religiously conscious of himself. As long as a person is in the state of melancholy, however, it holds no *meaning* for him; he can certainly describe his situation, but what makes him melancholy is hidden. Consequently, it is impossible for him to be cured. A cure can be brought about only by a breakthrough to religious subjectivity, of which his introversion is an anticipation. And only an extreme crisis of anxiety can occasion this breakthrough.

Once again, this description fits Kierkegaard's own spiritual evolution.[22] His inner unrest placed him "in the situation" propitious for accepting Christianity. As he himself recorded in his diary, what the modern Christian most lacks is a "painful situation to bring out the fact that one wants to become a Christian" (X² A 399). Without his interior suffering the essence of Christianity would have passed him by completely.

Let us, by way of example, consider one of Kierkegaard's most important religious categories in order to see the part played by his own experience in its discovery: the category of the individual. Kierkegaard first employed it because of his relationship with Regine Olsen, through which he became conscious of his solitude and his inability to communi-

---

[22] Only it would have been better in this case to call it a "sublation" —in the sense of a dialectical moment that is both preserved and transcended—than a "cure." With F. Geismar in *Teologisk Tidskrift* (1927), p. 192, and contrary to the psychologist P. A. Heiberg in *Søren Kierkegaards religiøse Udvikling* (Copenhagen, 1925), we believe that there was never a religious "cure" of Kierkegaard's melancholy. It never left him; it acquired a religious meaning.

cate with others. With this realization he set down his
message, written only for himself and for "the individual
whom with joy and gratitude, I call my reader" (ED III, 11:
LO I, 5; VIII A 430). When he first used this expression, he
was thinking only in terms of the one individual who could
understand his work (if not his whole psyche), Regine Olsen;
but with passing years, as the number of his readers was
approaching a "mass audience," this dedication became a
manifesto: his communication is always directed to the individual, because it forces every man continually to take a
strictly personal stand toward Christianity.[23]

And so "the individual" becomes a religious category, con-
ditioned by Kierkegaard's psychological isolation, but at the
same time transcending it as a universal determination of the
religious consciousness. In his *Point of View for my Work
as an Author* he regards this category as the most important
achievement of his work, the *sine qua non* of all religion.
This evaluation only confirmed the conclusion of previous
meditations in his diary:

This category is the point at which and across which God can
come to seize hold of the race. To remove that point is to de-
throne God (X[1] A 218).

Modern man has lost this notion. He sees everything historically and en masse. Christianity for him is an age-old
philosophy of life which over the centuries has proved itself
sufficiently that one need not commit himself personally to
it. Thus Christianity loses its transcendent value; it does

[23] "When I first used the category of 'the individual' in the Preface
to the *Two Edifying Discourses* of 1843, it still had for me, as well, a
personal meaning; the idea itself was not so very clear to me at the time
that, without this personal meaning, I would have employed it immediately. When I used it the second time, with greater force, in the
foreword to the *Edifying Discourses in Various Spirits,* then I realized
that what I was doing was completely ideal" (X[3] A 308).

not shock any longer, it becomes a necessary part of this world, just as the Incarnation is a necessary moment in Hegel's world history.

"The individual"—that is the decisive Christian category and it will be decisive also for the future of Christianity. The fundamental confusion, the original sin of Christendom, is that year after year, decade after decade, century after century, it has pursued the insidious purpose—just about half unconscious of what it did—of tricking God out of his rights as the proprietor of Christianity, and has got it into its head that the race, the human race, was itself the inventor, or had come pretty close to inventing Christianity (PV XIII 650-51 LO 135).

Everyone must rediscover himself as an individual alone before God. Christianity cannot be handed down in a tradition; every man who comes into this world must be shocked anew, and, in this shock, advance to faith or fall into despair.

II

THE DIALECTIC OF SIN

1. Kierkegaard's Dialectical Anthropology

KIERKEGAARD'S THOUGHT is in large measure to be understood as a Christian reaction against Hegel, and it is in the theology of sin that he became most conscious of the opposition between the Hegelian system and what he considered to be authentic Christianity.

For Hegel whatever is real is intelligible. He thereby allows no qualification which would set the human mind apart from the divine mind. Hegel's Spirit is one: it is both human and divine. In man's philosophy God becomes conscious of Himself as absolute. Consequently, all the data of revelation are to be integrated into this absolute philosophy: they are to be made intelligible. For Kierkegaard such a theological philosophy is a direct denial of the most essential element of the Judeo-Christian revelation: God's transcendence. God and man are separated by an eternal abyss. Whatever He communicates to us can, therefore, never be reduced to philosophical categories. The revelation can not be understood, it must be believed, that is, accepted on authority. This is particularly

the case with its primordial data that man is sinful and needs
redemption.

But there is another reason for Kierkegaard's opposition.
Whereas Hegel's whole philosophy is based on the ontological
argument that knowledge ultimately coincides with individual existence, Kierkegaard returns to Kant's premise that
speculation is forever restricted to the realm of universal
possibility and never reaches the strictly individual. But sin
is per se individual, as we will see later. Therefore, to understand it is to misunderstand it, since understanding transforms it into a possibility and possible evil is no evil at all
(X^2 A 436). Evil exists only as a reality, that is individually.
Hegel would admit that sin, taken by itself, is unintelligible;
but as a moment in the process of the Absolute, it becomes
highly meaningful and necessary. In his own dialectic, sin
is pure *negativity*, as the terms weakness, sensuousness,
finitude, and so on, indicate. Since negativity is the moving
principle in the dialectic of consciousness, sin becomes a
necessary moment in the evolutionary process of the mind.
This theory removes sin from its ethico-religious context, in
which man takes a stand against God by a positive act, and
places it in the domain of logic, where it becomes a necessary
antithesis. Without any further justification, evil is identified
with negativity. By this not very logical transition, sin becomes
a moment of an objective, logical universe.[1]

The only correct attitude of thought with regard to sin is
to renounce it, because it is unintelligible and no objective
speculation can ever make it meaningful.[2] With the notion
of sin we have left the sphere of objective thought altogether.

---

[1] "In logic they use the negative as the motive power which brings
movement into everything. And movement in logic they must have, any
way they can get it, by fair means or foul" (CD IV 316 LO 11).

[2] We do not recall ever having found a definition of what Kierkegaard
understands by subjectivity. He himself seems to believe that he is
being completely faithful to traditional usage. But it is quite evident

Sin exists only when man is *conscious of himself as sinful,* and this he can be only in the subjective part of consciousness where he finds himself related to the transcendent.

Yet, in order to manifest its unintelligibility, speculation may "situate" sin in its psychological context. This will never reveal what sin is *in itself,* but it shows *where* the mysterious transition from innocence to sin occurs. For this purpose Kierkegaard has in his two works on sin, *The Concept of Dread* and *Sickness Unto Death,* developed an anthropology which, in spite of idealistic influences, displays an extremely personal approach.

To be a man is to be in a situation to which one must actively respond. Human existence is a task to be accomplished, a duty to be fulfilled. Rather than a static and self-enclosed consciousness, it is an active relationship. However, the active relationship which constitutes man's essence is not primarily a relation to the world, as it is for Marx and some contemporary philosophers: it is a relation to oneself and simultaneously to God. For Kierkegaard, man consists of a synthesis of soul and body which dynamically relates itself to itself. This return upon itself constitutes the spirit. By the self-relatedness of the spirit man escapes being dissolved in each successive moment of time. He remains *himself* throughout this succession. Spirit thus posits a moment of eternity and, with it, an ultimate principle, an absolute. There are only two possibilities: either man's relation to himself is in itself the ultimate or it becomes absolute by implying a further relation to the ultimate. The first hypothesis is rejected

---

that Kierkegaard's *subject,* because of its fundamental opposition to the *object,* cannot be Hegel's *subject,* which in its opposition is identical with the *object.* Perhaps we must proceed further back in tradition, to a time when this identity did not yet exist. J. Brown in "The Subject in Kierkegaard" from *Subject and Object in Modern Theology* (London, 1955), p. 39, thinks that he finds that connection in Kant.

from the outset. The second makes man into a religious being. He becomes himself only by relating himself to God. The relationship with eternity constitutes his very essence as spirit. This religious determination distinguishes Kierkegaard's concept of man from that of all modern philosophy. God becomes the Axis around which turns the whole relation of the ego to itself; without Him I cannot be myself, I cannot be spirit. Only "before God" do I become a person. Together with the first relation, the spirit's relation to itself, is given the second, the relation to its Origin. In choosing himself man also determines his attitude toward God: he must either accept his dependence, or turn himself away from God. As long as he has not committed himself on this issue, he has not yet really become spirit.[3]

Anyone who has not discovered his existence "before God," is not yet a *person*. He still remains in the first of the three existential stages, the *aesthetic*. His life is a mere succession of moments, in which he literally loses himself at every turn. For the aesthetic man there is no present, because there is no absolute around which time can concentrate itself. Only the Absolute can create a *present* in which time comes to a standstill and escapes the mere flux of succession. Through the Absolute, time participates in eternity, the present that never passes. Every consciousness requires at least *some* permanence in order to be conscious, but the aesthetic consciousness does not reach the point where it becomes a real *present*. The aesthete never commits himself, and thus never becomes a *self*, since the self is essentially a choice, an active relationship to oneself. It is generally agreed that the aesthete lives for the

[3] In Kierkegaard's view of the person as implying an essential relationship with God, the Swedish bishop T. Bohlin sees the influence of Schleiermacher's notion of religion as *feeling of dependence* (Abhängichkeitsgefühl). However, he rightly remarks that Kierkegaard sees this religiousness as a *becoming*, whereas for Schleiermacher it is a *being*, a situation (*Kierkegaards dogmatische Anschauung*, p. 213).

joys of the present, but his present is a mere abstraction lying between the past and the future (which are no less abstract): it has no consistency whatever (CD IV 393 LO 77). He may well think that he discovers eternity in his aesthetic pleasure, but this is only an illusion of true eternity, a mere immanent projection altogether subject to the relativity that produced it, unable to give stability to existence.

This aesthetic sphere bears within itself the germ of its own destruction: the frustrated attempts of the spirit to affirm itself causes a strange anxiety, eventually leading to despair (EO II 202 LO 158). This explains the melancholy which overcame Nero after his orgies and made him afraid of a little child. Only a free decision can break through the aesthetic attitude. At this point it does not matter to what one commits oneself, since the dilemma here is not between good and evil, but between choosing and not choosing. If the aesthete has followed his attitude to its ultimate consequences, there is nothing left for him to choose other than the despair into which he has brought himself. If he accepts it resolutely, he chooses himself and thus brings an absolute element into his existence: in his commitment to despair he constitutes a relationship to himself (EO II 182-83 LO 142).

One does not fall into despair; one chooses it voluntarily. And in choosing despair man also chooses the object of despair, *himself*. This is an absolute, not subordinate to anything else (EO II 230 LO 179). The unique character of this absolute is that it becomes real only through choice, and, on the other hand, that it must already be real to be an object of choice. This is possible only if I am, myself, the choice, and if freedom is the very essence of my existence, for only then can I become myself through realizing my freedom. The fact that I am essentially *freedom* is at the origin of the paradox that I choose the most concrete reality, myself, and that this self becomes concrete only by that choice. In order to choose myself, I should already *be* myself: on the other hand, I become myself only in choosing myself (EO II 231-33 LO 179-81).

A comparison of this phenomenological description of freedom, given in *Either/Or,* with the definition of the person in *Sickness unto Death* and the *Concept of Dread,* with which we started this chapter, shows that they correspond perfectly. As a relation, the spirit is essentially dynamic; it must realize itself at every moment.[4] To relate oneself actively to oneself can only mean to choose oneself, to be free (TC XII 183 LO 159). Only when I realize my freedom is the relation to myself real; then I become spirit.[5]

By his definition of a person as a capacity for choosing oneself, Kierkegaard has put all the stress on the subjective side. Not what he decides, the object of choice, but the decision itself, constitutes the spirit.[6] Therefore the essence of spirit is not the objective, the universal, but the subjective. All the force of the spirit is in the will. "The more will, the more self. A man who has no will at all is no self" (SD XI 160 LO 43-44). The notion of person is primarily ethical: to exist is not a situation, but a duty to be accomplished in a situation. This task is never finished; it is not a decision once and for all, but one that, because of human temporality, should always be repeated. I am never spirit; I always become it. Man's choice is not restricted to a few important occasions; it is made from day to day (SD XI 243 LO 171).

In the choice of himself as an absolute, one leaves the aesthetic stage. Kierkegaard calls the new sphere, into which

[4] B. Meerpohl correctly observes that the object of Kierkegaard's anthropology is the *becoming* of man, not his *being.* Cf. *Die Verzweiflung als Metaphysisches Phänomenon in der Philosophie S. Kierkegaards* (Würzburg, 1934).

[5] L. Giess, *Liebe als Freiheit* (Temeschburg, 1939), p. 15.

[6] C. F. W. Anz, *Kierkegaard und der deutsche Idealismus* (Tübingen, 1956), pp. 30-33.

freedom has introduced man, the ethical. As soon as a person takes possession of himself and becomes free there arises an absolute distinction between good and evil.[7] For the speculative attitude, which Kierkegaard includes in the aesthetic (because of its lack of commitment), this distinction is only relative: good and evil can be integrated in a single system. The distinction becomes absolute when we make it so by a personal commitment. This means that good and evil are absolute only insofar as we will them. Such a statement does not reduce them to mere subjective determinations—they are objective and universal in themselves—but they become themselves only in the free decision of an absolute choice. Nothing but a conscious, personal acceptance can make objective standards into absolute values (EO II 242 LO 188).

Even in their subjective acceptance, however, the objective ethical standards are a limitation of the spirit. Kierkegaard proves this in his *Stages on Life's Way* with regard to what he considers the synthesis of ethical existence, the married life (SL VI 101-196 LO 95-178). To bind oneself in marriage is to commit oneself, and therefore to effect something absolute in life. But the question immediately arises whether a decision which fixes the spirit on a finite existence allows the infinite to come to full development; and whether the spirit is not obliged to remain only half-awake. The absolute of the ethical man is expressed in an existence which is extremely limited and, as such, relative. Although the synthesis of the ethical personality is more balanced than the

---

[7] How this distinction comes about will appear later. It originates in the morally evil act. But this does not mean that any fault necessarily brings a man into the ethical sphere. Good and evil can only acquire an absolute character on the ethical level. Therefore a fault on the aesthetic level can never formally be called a morally evil act, for the latter requires spirit, which is not constituted on the aesthetic level. On the other hand, a situation of spiritlessness is a refusal to be oneself, which is much worse than any actual moral fault.

aesthetic, which refuses to bind itself to the finite, the question remains whether the ethical man will ever be conscious of the absolute *as such,* which is the primary condition for becoming spirit. The very self-assurance of the ethical man makes his whole attitude somewhat suspect. "He feels no want of the eternal, for it is with him in time" (SL VI 123 LO 116).

Does this imply, however, that man may, or must, renounce the temporal? Does he have the right to bind himself by his own free decision so closely to the absolute as to exclude the relative? Is he allowed to abandon everything in order to belong to God alone? Can he withdraw from marriage and temporal duties to dedicate his life to the Eternal? The answer to these questions can hardly be affirmative. Renunciation of the temporal is indeed based on an ascetic attitude which repudiates everything that for a normal human being makes life worthwhile. Moreover, this complete detachment from ordinary life manifests an undue familiarity toward God.[8] Only a special vocation can justify such an exceptional life; a sign of such a vocation would be a physiological or psychological disposition which excludes a man from ordinary life. In this case God Himself has called him out of the normal course.

At any rate, it is certain that our relation to God has not yet received its ultimate form in the ethical decision. Religious and ethical categories do not coincide. This is illustrated in *Fear and Trembling* by the case of Abraham, who, through a special vocation of God, was ready to sacrifice his son Isaac, notwithstanding the fundamental ethical law: Thou shalt not kill. Does it follow that there is no relation

---

[8] We will see that Kierkegaard changed his opinion on this matter in his later writings; he came more and more to the conclusion that this ascetic life represents not the exception, but the most adequate expression of Christianity. Cf. SL XI 187 LO 170, and Mesnard, *Le vrai visage de Kierkegaard,* pp. 252-63.

between the ethical and the religious, and that the ethical stage is excluded from the religious? By no means, for the ethical man always places himself in a religious context; his choice of himself necessarily includes a relation to God. But this religious aspect remains more or less in the background; his relation to the infinite lies only *within* the finite.

The ethical decision, however, is not the last word. It leads necessarily to a crisis in which man will either despair again or turn to God. Up to this point God has been considered too exclusively as a complement of man's ethical life; he ordinarily recalls Him only in examination of conscience. By admitting his faults the ethical man expresses his essential limitation before God's transcendency and avoids falling into despair. Religious contrition thus belongs to the essence of ethical life, since it indicates that although evil is part of one's self, one detaches himself from it in his ultimate choice, and asserts his fundamental ability to observe the ethical law (EO II 242 LO 188).

At a certain point, however, my conscience will conclude that it is impossible to observe faithfully the claims of ethics, and I will be forced to abandon belief in my own basic righteousness. My conscience accuses me of being guilty before God not only in a *certain respect,* but in *every respect.* A new decision becomes necessary, in which I will either abandon myself to despair, or throw myself entirely on God's mercy.[9] Only in this moment can my commitment be called absolute, because only here do I choose my *self* completely, including the true relation to its Origin, guilt. "Only when I choose myself as guilty, do I choose myself absolutely" (EO

---

[9] Just as the aesthetic does not lead immediately into the ethical, the latter will never bring one automatically into the religious sphere; in neither case is there a gradual transition, but rather a leap of free will. Still, the ethical stage is the normal (not the necessary) preparation for the religious.

II 234 LO 182).[10] This means that the choice of myself, by which I escaped from the aesthetic stage, is only fully accomplished on the religious level, where I cast myself as totally guilty before God. The ethical stage was a transition. My decision becomes absolute only when it is completed in absolute despair or in absolute faith.

If the essence of spirit is subjectivity, it follows that man becomes fully spirit only in the religious stage. For in the ethical stage the subjective choice was still aimed at an objective realization of ethical values, whereas in the religious choice subjectivity abandons every hope of realizing itself objectively.[11] Man accepts himself as nonobjective, as an individual, completely isolated from the universal. He is alone with his guilt before God, and finds no place in an objective universe. But in choosing himself as guilty before God he finally chooses *himself* and his relation to the Origin of his self.

This decision "before God" brings a definitive structure into his existence. The flow of quantitatively distinct temporal moments concentrates itself in an *instant,* an eternal present which breaks into time and fixates it (CD IV 391-95 LO 76-80). In the religious stage eternity enters man's existence.[12] The spirit first becomes *real* on the religious level. Previously, the synthesis of the finite and the infinite (in which, as we saw, the essence of the spirit consists) was not yet accomplished, since the choice of myself on the ethical level was limited to the finite (though on a background of the

[10] It is true that Kierkegaard writes this about the ethical man in *Either/Or,* but at this point he has not yet discovered the religous as a completely separate sphere. Much of what he includes here under the ethical will belong to the religious in his later writings.

[11] Cf. H. Reuter, *S. Kierkegaards Religionsphilosophische Gedanken im Verhaltnis zu Hegels Religionsphilosophischem System* (Leipzig, 1914), p. 106.

[12] S. U. Zuidema, "Het Existentialisme bij Kierkegaard," *Philosophia Reformata,* 15 (1950), p. 54.

infinite). Therefore, only the religious man *exists* in the full sense of the word, that is, as synthesis of the temporal and eternity.

2. *Original Sin and Dread*

From the theory of freedom which we outlined in the previous section, and which supports his whole anthropology, Kierkegaard approaches the mystery of sin. All the emphasis here is on the free decision: to sin means to take a stand against God. This notion conflicts with every opinion that in any way minimizes the freedom of the sinful act, such as Hegel's doctrine of negativity, or Luther's teaching that man is born in the state of *unfreedom*.

For Hegel, the state of innocence before sin is the *immediate* stage in the developing consciousness of the Spirit. But immediacy is an abstract moment, which cannot exist in itself and which is real only insofar as it is annulled in an antithesis (CD IV 399 LO 32). Thus innocence becomes a prior moment of guilt, rational to the extent that guilt follows it of *necessity,* but possessing no reality of itself. The stage of reflection, at which knowledge commences, negates innocence and posits sin.

Kierkegaard agrees that innocence is ignorance (CD IV 342 LO 34). But this admission does not imply that ignorance *must* become knowing in sin; such an implication certainly does not follow from the definition of innocence. Moreover, knowledge through sin is not a perfection, but rather a degradation, as compared to the ignorant state of innocence. Kierkegaard readily accepts the statement that logical immediacy must be annulled, if indeed this is more than a tautology or an unnecessary explanation—for, after all, the immediate can never exist by itself and so has no need of

being annulled (CD IV 339 LO 32). But to equate innocence
with the logical category of immediacy seems a confusion of
ethics with logic. Innocence bears no resemblance to the
nonbeing of immediacy, which begins to exist only when it is
annulled, but is rather a complete, self-contained reality
(CD IV 341 LO 34). If innocence is annulled, this is the
result not of an immanent necessity, but of a transcending
leap into another reality.[13]

Kierkegaard denounces the same absence of freedom in the
orthodox Lutheran doctrine of original sin. If the Reformation Confessions are taken literally, he believes, original sin
caused such a substantial change in man that sin became his
very essence (CD IV 331 LO 24). While not denying that
original sin is fundamental, Kierkegaard is of the opinion that
such an inheritance theory deprives sin of the elements of
personal freedom and responsibility. The Swedish bishop,
Thorsten Bohlin, elucidates this point quite clearly:

In the doctrine of original sin of older orthodox dogma, he sees
a theory which, though it is the strongest possible expression of
the gravity of sin, in fact weakens and paralyzes man's struggle
against sin, because it accepts the occurrence of a radical change
in human nature as a result of sin.[14]

Orthodox Lutheranism cuts Adam off from the general
human condition and puts him outside the human race:
when his first descendants enter this world, their lot has already been definitively determined. It is no longer apparent
how one's personal sin can now have any relation to Adam's.
For Hegel, there is no original *sin* at all (a necessary evolution
is not sin). For Protestant orthodoxy, original sin is not
original, because Adam's sin has nothing in common with
our sin; his sin is a free act transforming innocence into sin-

[13] Cf. Reuter, *op. cit.*, p. 100, and Thust, *op. cit.*, p. 278.
[14] Bohlin, *op. cit.*, p. 107.

fulness, while our sin is a predetermined transition from sinfulness to sin. The word "sin" loses all meaning if, on the one hand, it signifies the cause of sinfulness (in Adam) and, on the other, the result of sinfulness (in us). That is why Adam's sin cannot be called an *original* sin. Only if there is true sin on our part, and only if there is a clear continuity between Adam and ourselves, does the concept of original sin make sense. In both erroneous theories, the present state of the human race begins *after* Adam.

To be sound, any interpretation of Adam's sin has to include the relationship between the first and all other sins. But it is incorrect to call this a cause-and-effect relationship, for in that case Adam's sin (which was free) would have an entirely different meaning from our sin (which is not free), and there would once again be no similarity between Adam's situation and that of the rest of the race. For a like reason, any attempt to explain original sin by reference to Adam's unique position as *caput generis humani* (CD IV 333 LO 27) is to be rejected.

The entire problem, then, is reduced to the search for some situation common to Adam and to us (so that he remains within the series), which at the same time allows us to explain a definitive change in mankind with the first sin. Kierkegaard believes that he has found the solution in the fact that man is "at once himself and the whole race, in such wise that the whole race has part in the individual and the individual has part in the whole race" (CD IV 332 LO 26).

This statement one would expect from Hegel rather than from Kierkegaard. Is Kierkegaard convinced of what he is saying here? Or is he only playing with words, and making the concepts purposely vague, to avoid the difficulty that sin results from an individual free act and at the same time connotes a superindividual link?[15] In that case his theory of

[15] Bohlin, *op. cit.*, pp. 123-24.

original sin solves nothing, because to explain this difficulty was, precisely, its principal aim.

There seems to be only one other solution left: the individual is codetermined, externally as well as internally, both by himself and by the history of the human race; but the latter determination is restricted to the situation *in* which freedom is realized, and does not eliminate the personal responsibility by which we bring forth reality from the possible (the situation).[16]

The determination of the individual by the race requires that the race be a real entity subsisting *in* the individual; otherwise the spiritual bond between Adam and his posterity is as fictitious as in the two positions that Kierkegaard has explicitly repudiated. This solution is unusually Hegelian for Kierkegaard, but it is the only consistent one and it is confirmed by an early diary entry in which he poses the problem in the same way:

Would not original sin, made possible by Adam's sin and real by his posterity (continuity of the race), that of which one reads in the *Epistle to the Romans* 5, 13, where it is said that all men have sinned in Adam, involve, if one adheres to the orthodox thinking of the Protestant churches and withdraws from the notion every pelagian reservation (not: *cum hoc non ideo propter hoc,* but *cum hoc et propter hoc*)—does it not necessarily involve the doctrine of the role of the Church, of its treasury of good works and of the benefits that it provides (according to the Catholics) as the only adequate counterbalance? (II A 117).

Kierkegaard's reference to "the treasury of good works" in the Church should not lead one to the conclusion that he accepts the doctrine of the Mystical Body of Christ; the chapters both on grace and on the Church will show how far

---

[16] E. Hirsch, *Kierkegaard-Studien* (Gütersloh, 1930, 1931, 1933), pp. 713-14.

removed he is from this position. For, like sin, grace is ultimately a strictly individual matter, and excludes any community with others.

Before attempting to define the essence of original sin, we must first answer the question of exactly why Adam's sin is so significant. If the only bond between him and ourselves is that of common race, then there is no reason why his sin should be more important than that of any other man. When Adam is deprived of the extraordinary position which ortho-dox dogmatics assigned to him, the effect of his sin is reduced to that of any other sin. Nevertheless, Kierkegaard himself admits that the first sin had greater significance—not be-cause of the nature of the sin itself, nor because of the per-son of Adam, but because of the qualitative change under-gone by mankind on account of the *first* sin.[17] Before this sin mankind was sinless, and afterward became sinful. No other, later sin will ever have the same consequences, because by this first transgression the entire human race became sinful once and for all. For this reason, the first sin is *the* sin (CD IV 334 LO 27). With it, sin came into the world.

The identity of the first man is entirely accidental; any first sin after Adam would have effected the same complete upheaval. Something similar happens in each individual life. Just as Adam's sin represented a leap into a new world, so the sin of each human being is a leap from relative innocence to sinfulness.

In order to maintain at once the relation of inheritance and the reality of personal responsibility, Kierkegaard tries to reduce original sin to a middle term, which on the one hand has enough in common with sin to be a link between Adam's sin and our own, and on the other hand retains enough of

[17] It is to be noticed that this qualitative change is not the same as the *substantial* change which Kierkegaard thinks is to be found in the oldest confessions of the Reformation.

the nature of innocence to make possible an explanation of the transition from innocence to guilt. This concept would reduce the difference between Adam and ourselves, before sin, to a difference of degree: a *greater* or *lesser* disposition to sin. Consequently, the first man remains a member of the series, and Adam's descendants still would be confronted with the same personal responsibility in sinning. Kierkegaard believes that he has discovered this explanatory principle in the concept of *dread*.

As early as 1842 Kierkegaard pointed out that dread is the fundamental category for understanding original sin (III A 233). Only this strange phenomenon, originating in man himself and yet limiting his freedom, can prepare for the unintelligible leap from innocence to sin. Dread by no means explains the leap, the sin itself (which by its very nature is unintelligible), but only the state of mind in which the unintelligible act is committed. Dread itself, therefore, is never sin.

In equating original sin with dread, Kierkegaard indicates that *original* sin is not a real sin; it is related to sin as a feminine principle—that is, it captures the contours of sin passively within itself. Consequently, the psychological concept of original sin does not account for the fact *that* sin originates; it only explains, once we acknowledge its existence, *how* sin originates.

We have already pointed out, in the previous chapter (p. 7), that dread, as distinguished from fear, is never dread of anything definite, but dread of our own unfulfilled potentialities. It is a dizziness of the spirit in the presence of itself. This dizziness arises from the fact that the spirit is still an abyss for itself, that it is not yet realized. In the state of innocence the spirit already is present, but only unconsciously. For this reason Kierkegaard, like Hegel, defines innocence as ignorance (CD IV 345 LO 37). The spirit dreams and, dreaming,

projects before itself its own possibilities as reality. But this
dream-reality is only a void full of possibilities. As such it is
both a hostile and a friendly power. Spirit tends to transform
the immediate relation between soul and body into a *conscious* synthesis. Its consciousness, however, endangers the
temporary, merely aesthetic relation in which soul and
body had found each other. As soon as spirit posits itself
as such, the primitive harmony between soul and body will
have to disappear. Therefore the conscious prominence of the
spirit constitutes a danger for the immediate synthesis.

This ambivalent relation between the fully conscious and
the semiconscious (that is, the hidden) states of the spirit is
what Kierkegaard calls dread, or anxiety. Thus anxiety is a
determination of spirit, the ambivalence of the finite spirit
that wishes to become itself and yet at the same time dreads
becoming itself, since in becoming itself it must lose itself.[18]

In dread, the *void* opens before the finite spirit as an abyss
within its own being, a cleavage in its existence. But this same
emptiness is the origin of its freedom. Freedom results from
the fact that the spirit is separated by an abyss from its own
reality (CD IV 346 LO 38).[19]

Originally it has nothing to do with the choice between
good and evil, for those categories are completely unknown to
the spirit in the state of ignorance. (That is why the for-
bidden tree in the second chapter of Genesis is called "the
tree of the knowledge of good and evil.") Possibility consists
exclusively of an indeterminate *being* able. A determination,
therefore, is required for the transition from possibility to
reality in which freedom realizes itself; good and evil cannot
accomplish this, since they do not yet exist. On the other
hand, a determination from without would destroy freedom

[18] Cf. Wahl, *Etudes Kierkegaardiennes,* p. 224.
[19] Cf. H. Urs von Balthasar, *Der Christ und die Angst* (Einsiedeln,
1954). Also M. Heidegger, *Was ist Metaphysik* (Freiburg, 1929).

itself. The only remaining explanation is that freedom, as pure possibility, determines itself. This is what happens in dread:

Dread is not a determinant of necessity, but neither is it of freedom; it is a trammeled freedom, in which freedom is not free in itself, but trammeled, not by necessity, but by itself (CD IV 354 LO 45).

In dread, innocence, as primitive ignorance of the spirit yet-to-be-constituted, reaches its apex: the semiconscious knowing of the spirit in its immediacy becomes acutely aware of its own unfulfilled emptiness. To dread is essentially to see the nothingness that is the very object of the *unknowing* recognized as ignorance (CD IV 348 LO 40). This focused ignorance is fraught with danger. Dread normally slumbers, but a single word is enough to awaken it and to make it concentrate its fascinated gaze upon this ignorance. That word has been spoken in God's command not to eat of the tree of knowledge.

Again, this should not be interpreted as if God's command stimulated the evil desire and thus established the proper disposition to sin. Such an explanation of sin by evil desire would be a *petitio principii,* for it presupposes the existence of evil before the original sin. If we even admit that Adam knew what sin was, then sin was already in the world, and the explanation assumes precisely the presence of the fact which ought to be shown. God's prohibition concentrated Adam's attention on his ignorance and thus awakened both dread and consciousness of freedom, the alarming possibility of *being able.* Psychology can go no further; what follows is an irrational leap, and thus inaccessible to psychology.

And so we arrive at the central point of this inquiry: the consequences of Adam's sin. Kierkegaard distinguishes two, which are intimately bound up with one another: that sin came into the world and that sexuality was posited (CD IV 353 LO 43-44). This does not mean that sexuality is sin, nor that there was no sexual distinction before sin. But before spirit consciously posited itself by choosing to sin, sexuality was present only unconsciously, and therefore, it was absent as *passion*.

The instant the spirit posits itself it posits the synthesis, but to posit the synthesis it must first permeate it differentially, and the extremest expression of the sensuous is precisely the sexual. This extreme man can attain only at the instant when the spirit becomes actual; before that time he is not an animal, but neither is he properly a man. The instant he becomes a man he becomes such only by being at the same time an animal (CD IV 353 LO 44).

As soon as the spirit affirms itself, it also posits the synthesis, and the cleavage between the two extremes of the synthesis becomes conscious. But this very consciousness provokes a new dread: from the opposition between soul and body originates a new possibility of freedom (in which dread essentially consists), for the synthesis reveals itself as necessarily dynamic and therefore to be realized again and again. The more this synthesis inclines toward either one of the two poles, the deeper grows the cleavage, and the more scope dread enjoys. It follows that, the more a human being is determined by sensuousness, the more its anxiety increases. Because she is more sensuous than man, woman is more inclined to anxiety, especially in the exercise of the generative functions, in which sensuousness takes complete possession of her.

After the fall of the first man, the sexual distinction became passion, and the history of mankind with sexual procreation began. The birth of all men since Adam by sexual generation has considerably heightened their anxiety. Indeed, it is in the

intense sensuousness of conception, when the spirit must withdraw completely and anxiety reaches its climax, that the new
individual originates (CD IV 378 LO 65).

Of course this new individual, like Adam in the state of
innocence, is a synthesis which must still receive its own
determination from its own spirit, but this synthesis is already a *derived* one—it flows from another synthesis—and
for this reason bears within itself the whole history of the
race. Precisely because Eve originated as a derived individual,
though not as the result of a sexual relation, dread is more
natural to her than to Adam. Thus it was Eve who led her
husband into sin. This does not imply that before the Fall
she had been less innocent than Adam. In itself, dread does
not involve guilt, because that would render inexplicable
how man is initiated into guilt through dread (CD IV 369
LO 57).

By pointing to their derivation from sex, Kierkegaard explains how in all later individuals the consequences of Adam's
sin could be transmitted through reproduction. In this respect
all other sins have the same consequence: with sinfulness,
dread increases, and with dread, the attractiveness of sin
to later generations. The only point that differentiates
Adam's sin from others, is that it brought sin *into a sinless*
world. This qualitative change in the human condition
(regardless of who Adam was and whether his sin would be
hereditary) was immediately reflected in the universe; when
Adam's sin made sensuousness into sinfulness, a shadow fell
upon the whole of creation (CD IV 364 LO 52).

To what extent now can the original sin, with which each
new individual enters the world, still be denominated *sin?*
To this question Kierkegaard's answer is very explicit: the
anxiety with which man enters this world, and which is increased considerably by the example of sin around him, is
no more qualified by good or evil than Adam's dread before

the Fall. In this respect each individual begins in the same state of innocence as Adam: the disposition to sin consists solely in a *quantitative increase* of dread. Therefore, every man who sins is just as responsible as Adam for the qualitative leap from innocence to guilt (CD IV 366 LO 54).

In this theory original sin is no longer a *sin*. Kierkegaard himself realizes how close he is here to Pelagianism. To defend himself, he makes a distinction between the individual and the race. In the species all sensuousness becomes sinfulness through Adam's sin, but in the individual it does not become so until he commits a personal sin. This means that, prior to one's personal sin, sinfulness is only *quantitatively* —which Kierkegaard defines in a parenthesis as "nonessentially"—present. There has been a greater tendency to sin from the moment the human race as such became sinful (CD IV 364 LO 52).

Within the framework of this merely quantitative sinfulness—this disposition to sin—does the word "guilt" still have meaning? Here again Kierkegaard believes that not to accept an original innocence in each individual is to abandon thought itself; inheritance would mean that an individual is a pure specimen of the species, whereas guilt indicates an autonomous determination by the individual (CD IV 366 LO 54). However strong may be the disposition to sin, it must always preserve the dialectical ambiguity it had for Adam, by which guilt comes into existence only through a leap (CD IV 357 LO 47).

After so many clear statements, one is somewhat startled to read, further on (1850) in Kierkegaard's diary, the following assertion:

Original sin is guilt—that is the real paradox! How paradoxical that is may best be seen thus. It is found by compounding qualitatively different categories. To "inherit" is a natural category;

"guilt" is an ethical and spiritual category. Now, who would ever think, says reason, of putting them together, of saying that something is inherited which by definition cannot be inherited? It must be believed. The paradox in Christian truth is invariably due to the fact that it is truth as it exists for God. The standard of measure and the end is superhuman and there is only one relationship possible: faith (X^2 A 481) (1061).

In this passage original sin is obviously regarded as a form of guilt. Is this contradiction to be attributed to an evolution in Kierkegaard's thinking on the subject? But if so, what explanation is to be offered of another entry (X^2 A 22) (967), which was written only a few months prior to this one and which remains entirely faithful to the opinion set forth in *The Concept of Dread?* Are we to say simply that Kierkegaard contradicts himself here? Perhaps, but another interpretation is possible on the basis of texts of the same period.

Commenting on Julius Müller's book on sin,[20] which he had read with the greatest attention, Kierkegaard asks himself where the *guilt* of original sin is to be located. Two elements are prominent: (1) guilt is where sin is, and original sin is real guilt insofar as all actual sins flow from it (X^2 A 472); (2) the guilt of original sin exists only in God's eyes, and this stems from the fact that God sees everything in *uno.* God sees *in each individual mankind as a race,* and there is no doubt but that mankind has become guilty and sinful through Adam's sin (X^2 A 421 and 473).

Leaving aside the first element, which is taken in its entirety from Müller, we note in the second that Kierkegaard makes a distinction between original sin in God's eyes and a merely human conception of original sin as *phenomenon* (that is, as it appears to us). In its essence sin can be understood by God alone and remains inaccessible to human speculation. The legitimate investigation of the psychological phenomena

[20] *Die Christliche Lehre von der Sünde* (Breslau, 1849).

which precede or follow sin exceeds the limits of its competence when it pretends to explain sin itself. There is nothing
to prevent psychology from dealing with the purely human
phenomena which sin causes in the human psyche, as long
as it prescinds from the essence of sin. But the fact that both
before and after sin, psychology discovers only anxiety and
no guilt, although Kierkegaard concedes—no doubt from
personal experience—that dread can sometimes take on the
appearance of guilt (CD IV 380 LO 67), does not imply that
sin is totally absent.

Even so there remain two basic obstacles in balancing this
explanation with the rest of Kierkegaard's theology: (1)
his often-repeated statement that man is always alone in the
eyes of God—a single individual; (2) his previous identification of sin with consciousness of sin. It would seem to me
that in his treatment of original sin Kierkegaard is laboring
with two concepts which he is unable to harmonize completely. In the quotation above he adheres to the theological
tradition that the original sin was truly sin. In *The Concept
of Dread* he is, despite his vehement objections, influenced
by Hegel, and original sin is no longer a sin. Most commentators agree that here he abandons the orthodox tradition of
the Reformation. Particularly, the thesis that man is no longer
free to do good and avoid evil since the Fall, seems to be
rejected. Indeed, if anxiety (that is, the essence of the original
sin) excludes freedom, then the fact of personal responsibility,
for the defense of which this entire theory was constructed,
would cease to exist. On the other hand, it cannot be denied
that the freedom of anxiety is also a form of bondage—but
a bondage into which freedom has led itself. To clarify this,
we must analyze the structure of the sinful act more closely.

3. The Structure of the Sinful Act

From the beginning we have distinguished dread from fear
in that the former has *nothing* as object (CD IV 410 LO 92).
Then how can guilt cause dread? Must guilt not be *something* definite, especially for a Christian, who through his
entire social and historical background knows exactly what
sin is? This very contention Kierkegaard will deny: a man
never knows what guilt is until he has sinned. It is only after
sin that guilt is no longer dreaded.[21] The only thing a man
can learn from others about sin is that it opens up a world
of unexperienced possibilities. As long as he is not personally
acquainted with them, he does not feel completely human.
Therefore, any information he receives about sin has no
effect other than to arouse anxiety. Everyone who has been
educated in Christianity knows from tradition that sensuousness means sinfulness, but, so long as he has not yet sinned
himself, this truth will carry no meaning for him. Like God's
prohibition in the Garden of Eden, it will serve only to
awaken or to increase his anxiety (CD IV 380 LO 66-67).

The greater the emphasis on sin, the stronger the anxiety.
That is why an over-strict education in Christianity is a
most dangerous occasion for sin. With the fascination of a
serpent's glance, anxiety allures one to sin (CD IV 410 LO
92).[22] It is evident that the disposition to become guilty has
here reached a quantitative maximum, which it did not have
in Adam's state of innocence. In the latter the possibilities
of freedom were exclusively determined by one prohibition,

[21] We will see later that sin brings him into a new dialectical relationship in which dread is not in the least diminished.

[22] Kierkegaard gives an elaborate example of this in his diary: how
the very dread of evil thoughts delivers one up to them (IX A 333)
(825). It is hardly necessary to point out the strongly autobiographical
element in this whole analysis of dread and sin.

whereas here are added, particularly by the example of others, all the specifications of the Christian notion of sin. Guilt receives an increasingly concrete aspect, whereby it becomes more and more *possible* to one's freedom. Eventually the whole world seems to conspire to make a man guilty (CD 417 LO 98). But all these occasions of sin cannot suppress freedom; they merely concentrate attention on what the innocent man experiences essentially as a void, a pure possibility of freedom. Therefore guilt must emanate from freedom itself.

It is the supreme glory of freedom that it has only with itself to do, that it projects guilt in its possibility and also posits it by itself, and if guilt is posited actually, freedom still posits it by itself (CD IV 416 LO 97).

Yet it would still seem that anxiety can never lead to guilt; for if guilt results only from freedom, anxiety which "trammels" freedom must diminish or eliminate guilt. Kierkegaard's answer to this objection is that man *allowed* himself to become anguished (CD IV 347 LO 39). Or, as he afterward puts it in his diary, man is responsible for his sin as a drunkard is guilty of getting drunk, although drunkenness itself is outside one's consciousness and therefore outside guilt (X^2 A 437) (1053).

However, it is not in the surrender to anxiety that guilt consists. Man becomes guilty only at the instant when, driven by anxiety, he surrenders to *sin*. The transition from innocence to guilt occurs in the fall into sin itself, and at that moment man is no longer free. Thus, in spite of all the emphasis on the freedom of the sinful act, Kierkegaard's concept of dread (the essence of original sin) appears to contain an undeniable element of necessity, which brings him closer to Protestant orthodoxy.

But has not sin at least freed man from anxiety? Evil arouses dread only until one has yielded to it; thereafter, there would seem to be no place left for anxiety. Concerning a past sin one can have only contrition. Nevertheless, some anxiety does remain, not only because of the increased sensuousness, but also as a consequence of the sin itself. For in the qualitative leap of sin not every possibility was actualized. As an unreasonable fact, sin immediately confronts one with a new decision: to persist in evil or to begin a new life. And so anxiety reappears in double form: anxiety over evil and anxiety over good.

The anxiety over evil can lead to further sin. In sin man has discovered his concrete possibilities for doing evil. He knows by experience that he is capable of sin, and this knowledge, in case he truly repents, can cause so much dread that a new fall is imminent. Moreover, dread can concentrate on the past as well as on the future. As we have already noted, it is true that contrition removes dread; but there is a form of remorse which, like the mad repentance of King Lear, tries to undo what has been done, and in its despair attempts to see the past again as possibility (CD IV 423 LO 102-3).

Even more dangerous is the demoniacal, or the dread of the good, which arises after sin. Just as the possibility of evil caused anguish to the innocent person, so now the possibility of good arouses dread in the sinner. In the state of innocence freedom had not yet asserted itself; in the state of sin freedom has given itself into bondage. In both cases the transition to a new state requires a new commitment which occasions anxiety. This commitment becomes particularly difficult for the spirit which has repudiated its Origin and consciously enclosed itself in the synthesis of soul and body as in a "lower self." After sin, man becomes afraid of his Origin, and tends to shut himself up in despair (SD XI 248 LO 178).

Shut-upness is for Kierkegaard the most adequate expression of evil:

The demoniacal does not shut itself up *with* something, but shuts *itself* up; and in this lies the mystery of existence, the fact that unfreedom makes a prisoner precisely of itself. Freedom is constantly communicating . . .; unfreedom becomes more and more shut up and wants no communication (CD IV 432 LO 110).

Kierkegaard finds this phenomenon in every form of unfreedom—from nervous hypertension to satanic unbelief (CD IV 446-50 LO 122-26). That is why the devil that Christ exorcises in the Gospel is dumb: in language lies the possibility of communication and liberation. That is also why at another time he cries out at Christ, "What have I to do with Thee?" (Mk 5, 7) and again asks Him to leave him alone (CD IV 433 LO 111). In these various forms of isolation appears the same dread of the good.

This is not the proper place to discuss Kierkegaard's treatment of the demoniacal, although it is one of the most remarkable studies ever written on that subject. Eventually the individual, after the dread of sin, must make a new decision. If he chooses faith, he is saved, and dread becomes grace. If he chooses despair, sin is decisively rooted in his life.[23]

Although we have defined sin as an essentially religious category, it only becomes entirely so in this second, definitive choice of despair. Sin arising from dread is still partly on the ethical level; the person who sins out of dread is at once guilty and not guilty. Only after sin does man fully know the difference between good and evil and experience himself as guilty before God. At this point he has to make a final decision: either he commits himself to God's mercy or he becomes obdurate in his separation from God and despairs.

[23] This decision is not necessarily made after the first sin; it is obvious from the preceding that man can stumble many times.

Despair is a refusal to live up to the task of existence, to become oneself.[24] Being a relation to eternity, the spirit is capable of constituting itself as a disproportion. The many possible forms of this disproportion all resemble one another in that they prevent the spirit from becoming itself, and the eternal from permeating the temporal. That is why Kierkegaard could define despair, as "the disproportion between *the temporal and the eternal* in man" (VIII B 168).

Although this refusal of the eternal is most explicit in its religious form, it is already present on the lower levels of consciousness. For example, the transition between the aesthetic and ethical stages was made by a choice of despair. This despair, like any other, was based *ultimately* on sin, but at that level it had not yet shown its religious character. The same is true for the spiritlessness of the aesthetic attitude: it cannot be called sin in the strict sense of the word, for the spirit has not yet asserted itself. Still, Kierkegaard calls it despair. Why? The spirit, in its dreaming state before reflection, feels an indeterminate dread of disturbing the unreflective harmony of the soul and body. Thus it is possible that the spirit does not dare to assert itself. As long as man perseveres in this state, he is immersed in a very dangerous sort of despair, for he refuses to be aware of being a spirit. Thus many have this "sickness unto death" without knowing it, but this does not mean that they are not responsible for it.

Here lies the whole difference between dread and despair. The man who experiences dread is not guilty; he who despairs is. Despair begins as soon as one yields to the baneful influence of anxiety and shuts himself up within himself. Or, to be more precise, despair in its first stage is the moment at which dread becomes guilt—not, as in the Fall, by a leap into evil, but by a refusal to make a leap at all. Before, we

---

[24] Meerpohl, *op. cit.,* pp. 42, 78.

saw that Kierkegaard describes dread as a dizziness (A IV 366 LO 55); in a preliminary study for *The Sickness unto Death,* he compares this dizziness with despair and concludes:

The despairing person, though he is like someone dizzy, who is not in control of himself at the moment of his dizziness, is, however, responsible for his being in despair, which cannot equally be said of someone who is dizzy (VIII B 168).

In dread, the spirit is not yet conscious. In despair, the individual has already determined himself to spirit, although this determination may sometimes consist in a refusal to be determined—obduracy in spiritlessness. Therefore, the despairing man is at every moment responsible for his despair; to be spirit involves freedom and thus responsibility as well. Despair is not a disease which, once contracted, must be suffered to the end; it is contracted as often as one posits the disproportion to himself (SD XI 147 LO 22-23).

This is paradoxical, since one form of despair consists in having no possibilities open (SD XI 169-70 LO 57-58). The absence of possibility would seem to exclude freedom, especially when one has defined the latter as pure *to-be-able*. But possibility, according to Kierkegaard, does not depend on external circumstances, as though only certain situations were hopeful and others hopeless. Man creates his own possibilities through *faith,* and faith begins only when there are no remaining human possibilities. For God everything is possible. When someone despairs of all possibility then he has lost God and himself as well (SD XI 172 LO 62).

Here we come to the very core of despair: it is always despair of oneself, and in the end despair of God. At first sight it might seem that one despairs only of a *situation,* but this is false. When an ambitious person does not achieve his goal, he despairs not because of his failure, but because of himself being involved in this failure (SD XI 150 LO 27). Despair can always be reduced to this pattern—man's *refusal to be himself,* his wish to rid himself of himself. True, there is also an attitude in which man wants *to be himself* in despair, but the contradiction is only apparent. For when a man in despair wants to be himself, he can do so only at the cost of breaking his relation with God (SD XI 144 LO 18). And if one wishes to be himself independent of that power on which this *self* depends, he desires to be that which he is not (SD XI 151 LO 29). Therefore, to accept oneself in despair is a refusal to be one's real self. It also follows that militant atheism is only despair of oneself. In a sense, it is the prototype of all despair; for if despair is a refusal to be oneself, it is implied that one wants to be oneself *against* God. For this reason, despair always has a religious origin, and every sin is ultimately (that is, insofar as it is religious) a sin of despair.

The identification of sin with despair raises many difficulties. We already mentioned the existence of despair on the aesthetic stage, where there is no actual sin. But there is more. On the one hand, Kierkegaard asserts that despair is a sickness which, outside Christendom, is universal: a pagan must necessarily despair because without revelation he cannot properly realize his dependence on God. He must despair because he cannot truly be himself (SD XI 153 LO 32). On the other hand, Kierkegaard has defined sin as despair *before God.* But since only a Christian has a correct concept of God, it seems that sin, in the true sense of the word, can exist only in Christianity. And this conclusion has been affirmed by Kierkegaard himself. Then how can sin and despair ever coincide, if the one exists only within, and the other only *outside of,* Christianity?[25]

Kierkegaard's solution, which raises still further problems,

[25] T. Bohlin has already posed this problem: *op. cit.,* pp. 215-17.

depends on his concept of *potentiality*.[26] Only the "potential-ized" despair which is grounded in a correct notion of God, such as the Christian possesses from revelation, is sin. Only the Christian acts with full consciousness of what he is doing when he shuts himself off from God; without this conscious-ness, Kierkegaard believes, no sin in the strict sense of the word is possible (SD XI 217 LO 129).

When a heathen becomes enclosed within his finite self he enters a state of despair (that is, a disproportion to himself) and of possible sin; but so long as he does not realize the true import of his act, this despair is not "potentialized." Now be-tween despair and "potentialized" despair there is as great a difference as between the natural and the revealed concept of sin.

Thus it appears that despair is completely different for a Christian than for a heathen, and that what the latter calls sin is from a Christian standpoint not yet true sin. This does not imply that Kierkegaard sets different norms for the sin of the natural man and that of the Christian. There is only one norm, full Christian consciousness. Until this is achieved, despair shares the objective structure of sin, but no more. And since sin is per se subjective, it is present here purely as a possibility. Besides, if despair were always true sin, which is per se conscious, how could there possibly be com-pletely unconscious despair?

One may be right therefore from a higher standpoint in regard-ing paganism as lying in sin, but properly the sin of paganism was the despairing unawareness of existing before God; this means to be without God in the world. On the other hand, it is for this reason true that the pagan did not sin in the strictest sense, for he did not sin before God (SD XI 217 LO 129).

[26] Kierkegaard uses "potentiality" to denote *power* rather than *capacity*.

Thus sin has become a conscious refusal to be onself before God, revealing itself in every possible shade of pride or weakness. All sins are identical in this respect, that they enclose man within himself. The state of sin, therefore, is a much greater evil than any actual sin. To sin may be a result of passion, but to remain in sin is always deliberate stubbornness (SD XI 245 LO 173-74).

In this state, too, there are several possible degrees. A man can despair about the fact that he has sinned: we met this strange, self-consuming remorse earlier, as anxiety after sin. To accept this anxiety is to despair. Not to forgive oneself is a greater sin than to have sinned. But it is even worse to despair of the forgiveness of sin, or to be scandalized by it, because in that case one is despairing directly of God (SD XI 253 LO 187).

Here it appears how diametrically opposed are faith and sin. In faith man abandons himself to God's mercy with certainty that his sins are forgiven. In offense he turns away and despairs. But only in the extremity of despair does sin manifest its full opposition to faith, when someone consciously rejects the very possibility of redemption. This is the sin against the Holy Ghost for which there is no absolution, because in it man closes himself off from God's forgiveness (SD XI 271 LO 215-16). Here sin and unbelief are identified. That is why Christ said that the Holy Ghost will convict the world of sin, "because they do not believe in Me" (Jn 16, 8-9; X[1] A 384). Not virtue, but faith, is the contrary of sin. "Whatsoever is not of faith is sin" (Rom 14, 23) (SD XI 219 LO 182). Hence it would almost seem as though we could return to the Socratic definition of sin as ignorance (cf. X[1] A 392). However, as the next chapter is intended to show, faith is not knowledge, but existential commitment.

III

JUDGMENT AND GRACE

1. The Suspension of Ethics

THE ROLE OF GRACE in religious existence is the problem with which Kierkegaard wrestled the longest. In 1838 he noted:

It takes a long time before one finds his way, feels at home, knows where everything belongs in the divine economy. One searches gropingly in a variety of moods, does not even know how to pray. Christ does not become a definite personality—one does not know what the assistance of the Holy Spirit means (II A 258).

Only in his later years did he come to feel that, by the whole detour of his life, he had discovered the true meaning of God's grace. It is perhaps because of this long search for grace that he wrote so little about its essence. It appears in his work as the unknown factor which is presupposed all the time, but it is recognized only at the end of his inquiry. Moreover, Kierkegaard is naturally more interested in the existential dimension of grace—its appropriation—than in its objective origination. And so he has placed all the emphasis on the subjective conditions for the reception of grace.[1]

[1] Thust, *Kierkegaard, Der Dichter des Religiösen,* p. 495.

Except in a certain *situation* man feels no existential need
for grace (X² A 284). Redemption is meaningful only to the
anguished conscience, not to the speculative philosopher who
sits comfortably behind his desk and dominates the world
in thought. What does hunger mean to someone who can
live without food? (VII A 192). Only an ethical existence can
lead us into this condition of necessity. Although, as Luther
rightly remarks, such indigence is itself already a grace, this
grace does not penetrate into our inner life, and "necessity"
remains an empty word, unless there is a serious and sincere
human exertion. Most people *feel* helplessness only during
the Sunday sermon; the rest of the time they feel quite capable
of managing by themselves (PS VII 458-59 LO 419).

It is not easy for a man to realize that he needs God and
that this need is his highest perfection. No external pressure
will ever be able to convince him of his inner helplessness.
Even when the whole world comes crashing down and crushes
him, he still harbors a vague suspicion that he would be able
to do something about it if the outside force were not so
great (ED V 109 LO IV 38).

Only a failure in the innermost depths of his own person
can persuasively reveal to him his true condition and put him
in the proper situation for experiencing God's redemption.
The failure of ethics must necessarily precede the coming of
grace. In his later years Kierkegaard became more and more
convinced that Luther, if not in his personal life at least in
his doctrine, did not attach sufficient importance to this preparation. The result has been that the modern Protestant
always succeeds in his ethical striving, because he has
"adapted" ethics to his own capacities.

Along with the growth of common sense there gains ground a
certain sort of human lore, the lore concerning what we men
actually *are,* in these times. . . . But how men *ought to be;* about

God's requirements, about the ideals—about this less and less inquiry is made in proportion as common sense increases (JY XII 496-97 LO 169).

But as long as man fails to apply ethics to himself with absolute seriousness, Christianity, with its doctrines of grace and forgiveness of sin, will never become serious for him. It will settle into the quicksands of mood and transitory sentiment. Before there can be any question of pardon, man must first try to fulfill the universal law imposed on him as man; otherwise, the redemption will have no effect.[2] God wills that the universal order, in which He placed man, be respected; therefore the particular order of grace must be preceded by an effort to fulfill the universal (VII B 235 p. 67). In spite of its universal character, God's law is at the same time strictly personal: God speaks to each man individually.

Only then is there sense and meaning and truth and reality in existence, when all of us, each personally, if I may say so, accept our orders at one place and then, each one personally unconditionally obey this same order. Since it is one and the same order, then to that extent one man might be able to learn it from another—if it was certain, or at least reasonably certain, that this other man would communicate it rightly. However, there would still be a confusion everywhere, as it is in conflict with God's order, for God wishes, for the sake of certainty and equality and responsibility, that every individual should learn the law's requirement from Him (WL IX 138 LO 96).

By the law Kierkegaard understands the Mosaic Law, and, in general, all ethical effort prior to the Gospel. "Ethics" com-

---

[2] That is what Kierkegaard finds wrong in the private revelations of Dr. Adler, the dismissed former minister of Bornholm: there is no ethical element in the entire story of his conversion, and so it remains merely a religious anecdote, without any deeper meaning (VII B 235, p. 196). We will discuss Kierkegaard's critique of Adler in Chapter VI.

prehends everything which is learned as a moral obligation, even, as we will see later, the moral precepts of the Gospel.[3]

As noted previously, the law, because of the strictly individual character of its obligation, is already religiously determined. Judge William, Kierkegaard's paragon of the ethical existence, in *Stages on Life's Way,* is a profoundly religious person. But the religious element in his life is subordinate to the ethical. As a preparatory phase of the religious, the ethical is at once determined by and preserves a certain independence of it.[4] For that reason ethics always keeps a certain autonomy, but it may never be detached from the theonomy to which it is per se subordinated. We find different conceptions of ethics in Kierkegaard's writing depending on whether this autonomous moment comes more or less to the fore.

In *Fear and Trembling* he wants to emphasize the opposition between the ethical and the religious and therefore adopts a Hegelian definition of ethics as that which has no telos outside itself, but is its own telos. Kierkegaard seems to be more concerned here to transcend ethics, which found its most autonomous expression in Hegel's definition, than to give his own view.[5] In his diary he explicitly rejects any

[3] That Kierkegaard's ethical stage cannot be simply equated with the Old Law appears from the outset. As early as 1836 Kierkegaard cites with approval Hamann's parallel between law and intellect: what is true for the one is also true for the other (I A 237). This would be difficult to understand if it were meant to refer to a merely Biblical idea of law. By the word "law" in that first moment, therefore, is to be understood any ethics before the religious stage proper.

[4] This also sheds new light on Kierkegaard's three stages: they are not to be considered merely as chronological stages, but rather as an application of Hegel's dialectic to a Christian philosophy of life. As dialectical moments, they are so intrinsically linked with one another that they only receive their ultimate meaning from the whole, which is determined by the final, the religious moment.

[5] W. Bauer, *Die Ethik Kierkegaards* (Jena, 1912), p. 14. Hirsch also rejects any equation of Kierkegaard's idea of ethics with the Hegelian

autonomous morality that reposes immanently in itself. Man cannot be his own law, for we cannot be more severe as law-givers than as subjects of the law. A completely autonomous law is as fictitious as the beating Sancho Panza gave himself with his own hands. Law, by its very essence, must be given and enforced by a higher authority (X^2 A 396) (1041). An immanent law lacks the personal (and therefore also the religious) element which is basic for the ethical obligation.

According to Kierkegaard, the ethical obligation is per se transcendent: it is a task imposed on man, rather than an immanent self-realization. That is why the ethical stage in *Either/Or* and in *Stages on Life's Way*, where he gives his own view, is less autonomous and more religious. In ethics man accepts the reality of his personal existence and attempts to weave a God-given ideal into the very reality of this existence (CD IV 320-21 LO 15).

Kierkegaard regards ethics as essentially a sphere of transition, which brings man into contradiction with himself and thus leads him to the edge of the transcendent.

In ethics the individual starts the process of interiorization by choosing *himself*, thus transforming objective into subjective existence; but in the preservation of his finite self, which is essential for the ethical attitude, he again seizes upon objectivity. As long as he fails to abandon this, the road to pure subjectivity remains blocked. Despair of himself,[6] the consciousness of moral inadequacy, will remove this last bond

---

definition quoted by Johannes de Silentio in *Fear and Trembling* (*op. cit.*, p. 689).

[6] As the reader has probably noticed, we use the word "despair" here in a different sense from that of the second chapter. There it meant a turning away from the transcendent either by an acceptance or by a rejection of one's own disproportionality. Here it simply refers to that point at which a man becomes conscious of this disproportion and at which, because of his own insufficiency, he will have to make up his mind either to accept the transcendent (faith), or to refuse it (despair in the strict sense).

with the objective and force him into a dialectic of complete interiorization. To transgress the ethical law—and everyone must transgress it—is to act in opposition to one's true self. And so ethics in the end destroys itself in the contradiction which is consciously posited in despair. Only when one both chooses oneself and also abandons oneself in despair, has one decisively renounced all objective certainty and reached pure subjectivity (PS VII 239-40 LO 227). Henceforth, the only criterion of authenticity is interiority.

The complete abandonment of objectivity is so heavy a task that only despair can bring man to it. To bring about this despair is, according to Kierkegaard, the *raison d'être* of ethics. Such a conception is in stark contrast with a eudae-monistic attitude, which through an ethical life hopes to find happiness (CD IV 321 LO 15). Yet ethics, for Kierkegaard no less than for the eudaemonist, is a necessary step in the realization of man's true nature. But its influence is entirely negative (SL VI 458 LO 394). As soon as the crisis has been reached, ethics in its positive aspect becomes a temptation, the temptation to cling to "something positive" in life and thereby to avoid the risk of infinity. Ethics, at this point, must be *suspended*.

Lest the negative-religious approach to ethics become superficial, we must determine precisely why Christianity rejects the possibility of an ethical life as such. Is it because of the limitations of all human striving? Certainly not, because this was a fact as well known to pagans as to Christians. Besides, an imperfect fulfillment of ethical requirements leads, not to a suspension of ethics, but to more intensive striving to become "ethical." The real basis is the very state of man which Christianity reveals, a state so opposed to every ethical pursuit of the good, that the longer one remains in this state, the further one is from the ideal (PS VII 253 LO 238).

We recognize, in this fundamental orientation toward evil, the reality of sin with which the previous chapter was concerned. Consciousness of sin reveals man's true essence and thus prepares his relationship with the Absolute. For only truth can found a true relationship with the Absolute, and the truth about man is that he is a sinner. A being whose very existence is sin can only approach the Absolute, paradoxically enough, by the *distance* of his realization of guilt (PS VII 518 LO 470). An attitude of contrition alone maintains the Absolute in its full transcendence and, consequently, in its Absoluteness.[7]

At the end of this section it should be remarked that contrition only temporarily suspends ethical striving. Ethics has been *sublated,* in that term's *twofold* meaning of being suspended and of being preserved, on a higher level. We shall see later that, far from being destroyed by the new religious life of grace, ethical striving attains its fulfillment only on a religious level.

[7] The necessary opposition in which absolute transcendence maintains itself against even the very highest ethical order, is demonstrated to us in the story of Abraham, who was about to kill his own son at God's command. "By his act he overstepped the ethical entirely and possessed a higher *telos* outside of it, in relation to which he suspended the former. For I should very much like to know how one would bring Abraham's act into relation with the universal, and whether it is possible to discover any connection whatever between what Abraham did and the universal . . . except the fact that he transgressed it. It was not for the sake of saving a people (like Jephta), not to maintain the idea of the state (like Brutus) that Abraham did this, and not in order to reconcile angry deities. . . . Why then did Abraham do it? For God's sake, and (in complete identity with this) for his own sake. He did it for God's sake because God required this proof of his faith; for his own sake he did it in order that he might furnish the proof" (FT III 122 LO 88-89).

2. *Consciousness of Sin: The Way to God*

In the first moment of religious existence—Kierkegaard calls it "religiousness A," a pre-Christian but authentic form of religiousness—ethical contrition becomes religious *consciousness of guilt.* Man discovers a disproportion between his own existence and its transcendent origin. He finds himself guilty before God. In spite of its transcendent term, however, this relation remains essentially immanent. Indeed, man of *himself* is aware of his negative relationship to transcendence. *He* feels guilty—before the transcendent, it is true—but still in such a way that the feeling of guilt arises only from himself. The subject before and after guilt is one and the same: evil has not so corrupted him that he has essentially changed through his guilt. The relation to the Absolute subsists in the consciousness of guilt; it is simply recognized as different from what it was before (PS VII 522 LO 473-474).

On the contrary, consciousness of sin, which is essentially a datum of revelation, introduces a chasm into one's existence and makes one's religion transcendent. From divine revelation the subject learns that from the very beginning he has broken with the transcendent origin of his personality, and that he is born as "an other," a living contradiction of himself. On his own, man would never reach such consciousness of sin, because he is incapable of seeing himself as *another*; to see this presupposes a higher consciousness, comprehending the two irreducibly diverse moments. Without God's revelation no consciousness of sin is possible. In order to become conscious of his fall, man needs an intervention of the transcendent.

That is why Luther teaches so correctly that man must be told by a revelation of the full depth of sin in which he lies, and that the anguished conscience is not something that comes naturally, like hunger (VII A 192).

Thus any doctrine of justification by works is, from the beginning, excluded from the life of grace. Man can do nothing by himself; he cannot even realize that he is a sinner in need of grace, for this also is grace. Without a true realization of one's sinful condition, salvation becomes impossible. That is why heathenism was more in need of the revelation of sin than of the gospel of salvation. Consciousness of sin, which necessarily precedes redemption, is the first grace, and the necessary condition of all subsequent grace. For this reason, Christianity alone, however much in opposition with natural categories, reveals the true, the sinful nature of man.[8]

This direct intervention of the transcendent distinguishes Kierkegaard's thought from every idealistic philosophy of religion. His dialectic does not find its determinations in itself, but receives them from above. The negative moment of sin is not an immanent self-negation, but God's own denial of man.[9] What man learns by revelation is not a keystone but a stumbling block for reason. By himself man is unable to realize his total corruption: he is so immersed in it that God alone can reveal to him his true nature (X A 322). In this revelation man discovers not only the center of his own existence, but also Him to Whom that existence is related.[10]

In the previous chapter we learned that *person* means *spirit* and that spirit is a relation to oneself. It also is a relation to that which constitutes the relation, to God. But only consciousness of sin makes the relation to oneself into a *conscious*

[8] See also Hirsch, *Kierkegaard-Studien*, p. 688.
[9] See also Wahl, *Etudes Kierkegaardiennes*, pp. 146-47.
[10] "The feeling of guilt places man 'before God', and on the other hand, to be before God is only to be conscious of one's sin, of the infinite distance which separates us from God." Wahl, *op. cit.*, p. 358.

relation to God, for the consciousness of a disproportion implies that in reference to which the relation to oneself is disproportionate. Thus consciousness of sin, the beginning of religious experience, brings a new determination into the conscious living of being-a-person.[11]

Any immediate nondialectical relation with God is *ipso facto* false.[12] Religion must have a negative beginning in man's sinful state (IX A 32, 242).[13] The negativity of the consciousness of sin is necessary for the proper relationship with God. Even Socrates understood this to a certain extent: that is why his daimon gave him only negative advice (IX A 242). But he was the only man in antiquity who had this dialectical relationship with God. What paganism most lacked, and what makes Christianity an absolute religion, is the latter's conception of man as sinner (V A 16). Consciousness of sin is the *conditio sine qua non* for true Christianity (V A 10) (479).

So it is in the final analysis the consciousness of sin which binds man to Christianity. Whoever is not bound in this way is not bound in a Christian way (IX A 31) (820) [our translation].

[11] Cf. R. Guardini, "Der Ausgangspunkt der Denkbewegung S. Kierkegaards," *Unterscheidung des Christlichen*, pp. 469-72. Also L. Giess, *Liebe als Freiheit* (Temeschburg, 1939), pp. 20, 39.

[12] Kierkegaard acknowledges the possibility of a relationship with God stemming from immediate consciousness, as V A 8 clearly shows. However, this relation is not correct, because it leaves out the most fundamental element of a true relation with God: that I am a sinner and am therefore related to Him in a negative way. On this point, cf. W. Sperna Weiland, *Philosophy of Existence and Christianity* (Assen, 1951), p. 43, note 80.

[13] This is not to deny the positivity of sin, which we discussed in the preceding chapter. Here we are dealing only with contrition—and contrition is undeniably *negative*. It is also to be observed that the beginning of this dialectical evolution is a negative one only because of the historical fact of the Fall, not because of any logical necessity; otherwise sin would again become a necessary fact and the state of innocence an abstraction, as in Hegel.

This negativity is not a transitory stage in the religious experience, it is inherent to religion as such. All the positive elements in man's relationship with God will be "constantly wrapped up in the negative" (PS VII 514-15 LO 467).[14]

Thus we see that the first act of the redemption is the revelation of sin. While sin alienated us from God, consciousness of sin returns us to Him (VIII A 284). Only in this negative way does man really come into the presence of God. The consciousness of being a sinner before God is also the first step toward the realization of one's true self. He who does not know himself "before God" does not know himself to the full (CD X 54 LO 43). God clarifies man to himself; only before God does he realize the infinite meaning of his existence and become fully committed to it.

Before God man is per se alone. As personal and intimate as the consciousness of sin itself is the relation that originates from it. Indeed, in contrition man isolates himself from all others.

It is always only as an individual that one can have the truest relationship with God; for we always have the best idea of our own unworthiness when we are alone (IX A 318).

Nevertheless, this isolated existence becomes a very hard task. Man knows himself to be separated from God, and the more religiously he lives, the more oppressive becomes this idea. The relation to God cuts all social ties and throws man back, hopeless, upon himself. Indeed, although in one's innermost existence God reveals Himself so that one can exist only before Him, He reveals Himself as the one before Whom man is always guilty, the wholly Other before Whom man must disappear (VII² B 235).

[14] It is probably useless to remind the reader how great an influence Kierkegaard's idea of negativity has had on present-day dialectical theology.

Every step forward in man's relation with God is a step backward (X² A 642). The true experience of being before God never grows into a mystic sense of participation: it remains a feeling of fear and trembling. So long as man has not learned to tremble before God's Face he knows neither God nor himself. But to learn this he must have the courage to be alone.

True wonder and fear appear only when he . . . comes to be alone with the Omnipresent (ED V 217-18).

Therefore, to become a "single individual" is the most important task of authentic Christianity, for it is only as an individual that one is able to be in a true relationship with God (IX A 318).

Catholicism has realized this truth in the isolation of its cloisters and hermitages. Protestantism has abandoned monasteries, but it could certainly make fruitful use of them once again. The cloister is a true expression of Christianity. Even if modern man is no longer able to imitate this monastic life in its medieval form, he nevertheless ought to keep himself in a state of interior isolation before God (VIII A 126).

But before the terror of God's presence, man is inclined to take refuge in a community, which introduces a certain mediating element between the pressure of His presence and one's self (IX A 316). Social life will always be a temptation for the religious man. God has made a concession to this weakness of ours by addressing Himself to the entire human race. But it becomes irreligion when man regards this concession as the ideal religious relation, when he makes the community the center of religious worship. For thus he weakens the tension of qualitative distance which is the very essence of his relationship with God.

Modern man wants to reach God only through the mediation of a universal objective society in which he has no individual responsibility.[15] The center of gravity has become the impersonal power which mediates between God and man. Man feels himself supported by an entire society; he is no longer alone in his unworthiness before God. Even if he is unworthy as an individual, in society he is sure that he is much closer to God, and the infinite distance no longer seems to exist.[16]

If only there are many of us engaged in it, it is not wrong; what the many do is the will of God. . . . The thing to do is to become many, a whole lot of us; if we do that, then we are secured against the judgment of eternity (SD XI 263 LO 202-03).

This attitude undermines the basis of Christianity and of every true religion. Kierkegaard considers the replacement of the qualitative distinction betwen God and man by quantitative considerations, as the cause of all the current confusion (VIII A 414). There is only one remedy for this danger: to recall man to the full consciousness of this distance, and to bring him back to his eternal responsibility as an *individual* in the *present*. So long as he tries to measure his relationship with God in terms of objective standards of society and history, he misunderstands it. God is present only *to me*, not *to us*.[17] History, the objective standard par excellence, is totally inept to evaluate religion, for it knows only results and judges by the past, whereas one's relationship with God is realized in the *present*, in a decision determining the individual's stance in respect to God (IX A 112) (783).

[15] This modern attitude received its purest expression in Hegel's idealism, where religion acquires its definitive value only through the objective Spirit. Man becomes himself insofar as he participates in an objective community, and the objectivity of *history* alone will pronounce a final judgment about his relation to God. *Vorlesungen über die Philosophie der Religion* (Jubiläumausg.), p. 74. (X² A 439) (1054).

[16] See Anz, *Kierkegaard und der deutsche Idealismus,* pp. 34-35.

[17] III A 39. For the category of the individual see also Chapter I.

As soon as religion leaves the existential *present,* in which it is
pure actuality, it immediately becomes blunted (X¹ A 383).

The qualitative abyss between the solitary sinner and God
is for Kierkegaard the basic fact of Christian life. That is
why his theory of justification starts with such great emphasis
on God's judgment. Man's first encounter with God is that of
a guilty defendant before his Judge. Primarily, God's Word
does not signify redemption, but rather judgment and condemnation (IX A 322). In the *Postscript* Kierkegaard describes man's response to the divine judgment as the perma-
nent awareness of an indelible guilt in the sight of God, an
absolute guilt beyond quantitative ethical distinctions (PS VII
541 LO 489). By being a *man,* one is a sinner before God, regardless of his moral life. In an appendix to *Either/Or,*
Kierkegaard's pseudonym, Victor Eremita, had already
proved that before God we are all equally guilty. In the
destruction of Jerusalem children were punished for the sins
of their parents, and Christ Himself said that the Galileans
who were executed by Pilate had been no greater sinners than
other Jews.

The one element in sin which superficially seems most
personal, namely, that one's moral behavior has been worse
than that of others, recedes into the background as the consciousness of sin becomes more acute, and thus more truly
personal. In contrast with the qualitative abyss between God
and oneself, even the greatest quantitative difference is negli-
gible. As *men,* we are on the side of injustice, no matter how
we compare with other men. Hence it follows that man must
never attempt to explain why a particular punishment is
meted out to an individual, because the qualitative distinction between God and ourselves precludes any such explora-
tion. The only suitable attitude is found in Job's rejection
of all ethical explanations. To account for Job's adversity by

the greater magnitude of his sin leads to inconsistencies. From a human point of view Job is innocent and God is unfair to him; however, from a transcendent standpoint, Job is in debt to God. Job's friends reduce the distinction between God and man to a quantitative ethical distance. Only Job himself realizes that the qualitative abyss between God and man is the real issue (R III 269-73 LO 125-31).[18]

3. The Gospel of Suffering and the Instant of Grace

The qualitative abyss between God and sinful man increasingly occupied Kierkegaard's attention. This development reached its culmination in *The Gospel of Suffering* (the second part of the *Edifying Discourses in Various Spirits* [1847] ED VIII), where suffering becomes a source of religious joy. Only under the burden of suffering does man realize his guilt before God. Suffering, therefore, is the most essential category of religion. But in order to acknowledge it as such, man must withdraw into the proper sphere of religion, *interiority*. As long as he has not done so, suffering will always seem more or less accidental and meaningless (PS VII 275 LO 256). The aesthetic and the ethical man know only adversity, not suffering. Authentic suffering begins with consciousness of sin. There is a mutual causality between these two: consciousness of sin creates the interiority in which suffering originates; conversely, in consciousness of sin, suffering causes the internal tension which initiates the dialectic of interiorization (VIII A 85). Suffering compels man

[18] *Suffering*, which here manifests the distinction between God and man qualitatively potentialized by sin, will return in a further stage as *trial*. Kierkegaard does not make that distinction in *The Repetition*, because both categories proceed from the same qualitative distinction between God and man—the former *before*, the latter *after* redemption.

to abandon his immediate existence and sets him on the path
toward interiority.

It would be wrong, however, to suppose that after this
initial stage, suffering will disappear: it follows the general
law of negativity in the religious dialectic and increases as
interiority increases. Therefore one must not expect relief of
one's pain from religion. Religion consoles only by announc-
ing, in every instance of suffering, even greater suffering to
come (PS VII 428 LO 393). With increasing interiority there
is a heightening of internal tension, so that each stage of the
existential "pathos" (in the twofold meaning of suffering and
passion) seems to shrink almost to nothing in comparison
with what is yet to come. Christianity suppresses suffering
only by regarding all pain as unimportant in view of religious
pathos (IX A 147) (792).

If suffering has a religious significance, is it itself a mark
of election? In Kierkegaard's life this seemingly abstract
problem acquired a very concrete meaning. Did his *thorn in
the flesh* indicate that he was among the elect? If this thorn
consisted primarily, as he seems to imply, of a "need of the
spirit" manifesting itself in a feeling of despair, the question
becomes particularly intricate, because, as we saw in the
second chapter, despair always presupposes sin.

In his *Discourses of 1844,* Kierkegaard devotes a meditation to the religious meaning of St. Paul's thorn in the flesh.
He first warns the reader against superficiality: adversity is of
itself certainly no mark of election. "Has God ever made a
covenant with a man about external matters?" (ED V 120
LO IV 53). By "thorn in the flesh" Paul meant an interior
suffering, which followed the grace of mystic rapture. After
each ecstasy, the Apostle returned to himself only to discover
that he was still the sinner he had been before his conversion.

The same happens to any man who goes through a profound religious experience: at times he will relapse into his

old self. The feeling of despair in these relapses creates deep
spiritual distress, but it has a religious significance, for it pre-
vents man from presuming familiarity with the divine. That
man may be kept in fear and trembling, the greatest grace is
always accompanied by the direst danger (ED V 136 LO IV
73). If the divine involved only what is higher, man would
soon ascribe it to himself; consequently, it also has a lower
aspect, abasement. Of this, despair is the most terrible form.[19]

The danger for the religious man who lives in the absolute religion is, of course, meritoriousness; the danger that instead of
piety, he takes on abnegation, considers himself better than others
or attributes merit to himself before God, or at least holds the
self-satisfied conviction that he has done his duty.

Therefore, a religious man of this type usually has a secret sign,
such as Paul's thorn in the flesh, which gives him the courage to
stand firm, simply because that sign indicates to him his own
nothingness (X[1] A 72).

Thus we are able to answer the initial question affirma-
tively: suffering, even in its most abasing form and when
most conducive to alienation from God, is a mark of election
and is as dialectical as Christianity itself. Just as election and
rejection are inseparably linked, so all real suffering is a sign
of simultaneous condemnation and pardon. The horror of
Solomon's dream the night he discovered that his father was
a sinner, consisted in the contradiction that God is not the
God of the just, but of the God-forsaken, and that a man
must be God-forsaken in order to be one of God's elect (SL
VI 266 LO 237). Christianity can only bring redemption to
sinners; that is why every election implies a rejection. If one
presumes to classify himself definitively under either of
these categories, he excludes the dialectical relation between
God and man, and with it Christianity itself. No criterion

[19] Thust, *op. cit.,* pp. 511-12.

can ever offer us a *static* certitude of election that Christianity itself does not possess.

Suffering prefigures redemption in that it is a symbol of sin. Only suffering can teach us concretely that we are sinners, and sinners alone are capable of redemption. In that sense suffering is a token that one is *fit for eternity* (ED VIII 399 LO 57). But it is not a grace which *guarantees* election; it becomes a grace only insofar as one is able to profit from it. This means that suffering is at the same time a task. The twin aspects of grace and task are united so closely as to be mutually constitutive.

Suffering is at once the God-given grace of the only way which leads to a deepening in our relationship with God . . . and the God-given task of following the way by which, in an ethico-religious manner, we, as believers, are to learn what we must learn from Christ.[20]

What, then, will man learn through suffering? The answer to this question is deceptively simple to the understanding, but it makes heroic demands on the will: man must learn to *accept* his sufferings. Suffering is the feeling of eternity straining to break through time. To accept one's sufferings is to render himself accessible to the eternal and to leave the temporal to God.[21]

This theory is far removed from "Christian humanism," but no farther than Christ's pronouncement in the Gospel (VIII A 415) (713). Moreover, its severity is due not to divine cruelty, but to man's sinfulness. If eternity is to penetrate sinful human existence, it must do violence to temporality.

[20] Hirsch, *op. cit.*, p. 865.

[21] Kierkegaard develops this idea magnificently in *The School of Suffering*, a meditation on the text of Hebrews 5, 8: "Though he was a son, yet learned he obedience by the things which he suffered." Obedience here means total surrender to God's will (in suffering) (ED VIII 390-406 LO 47-64).

The "cleavage" of suffering is only an expression of the cleavage between time and eternity within fallen man. However, suffering in itself, although an effect of sinfulness, is not evil.[22] He who accepts it frees himself from the oppression of the temporal and opens himself to the eternal. Suffering liberates man from this world, so that he is able to discover eternity. This alone explains Christ's predilection for the crippled and the weak, the blind and the leprous: not that Christianity is a religion of compassion to be shared by only an unhappy few (VII A 143), but that "suffering is the qualitative expression of disparity [of man] with this world" (X[4] A 600) (1262). To accept this cleavage is to admit one's sinfulness and to open oneself to redemption. For this reason suffering is a necessary moment in the dialectic of grace: in our distress, we feel in our own bodies the need for redemption. Consciousness of sin as transgression of the law here becomes an existential need for God.

As a result of his suffering, man craves forgiveness of his sins at any cost; this becomes his sole interest. So long as consciousness of sin has not taken the form of suffering, one does not yet truly feel the need for redemption. In his meditation about the penitent woman of the Gospel, Kierkegaard provides us with a most impressive description of this need for redemption. Suffering from the consciousness of her sins, this woman was oblivious to all else.

To the sinful woman . . . everything had become indifferent: the hostility of the environment, the protest of the banquet, the opposition of the Pharisees or their cold derision—the place indeed was an impregnable fortress, just so defended as to make her entrance impossible, if everything else had not become indifferent to her. . . . And yet, she dared this because one thing was absolutely important to her: to find forgiveness (DC XII 300 LO 265).

[22] Each of the seven *Joyful Notes in the Strife of Suffering* (CD X 111-87 LO 95-163) ends with this sentence: "Sin alone is man's ruin."

Christianity consists in the belief that God has forgiven each of us through His Son, but unless one is in a situation of extreme *need* for forgiveness, doubt and fear of Christianity's exacting claims will be a deterrent. Christianity betokens the death of the natural man. One seeks redemption only if one has been so deeply shaken by sin that there remains no salvation in this world (X^1 A 279). As long as a man has not arrived at this consciousness of sin through deep suffering, in which he becomes completely detached from this world, he is unprepared for redemption.

If you are not conscious of your sinfulness to the extent that, in the most terrible anxiety of conscience, you dare not act otherwise than to cleave to Christ, you will never be a Christian. Only the torture of the consciousness of sin could account for a man's subjecting himself to this radical cure. To become a Christian is, among all, all, the most terrible operation. No more than a man who feels slightly indisposed would ever get the idea of subjecting himself to the most painful operation, would it ever enter one's head to concern himself with Christianity, if sin did not infinitely torture him (X^1 A 190; cf. also VIII A 47).

For most people the real difficulty, which only suffering can remedy, lies in the fact that they do not feel "sick" enough to accept Christianity (X^3 A 184). For the same reason most baptized Christians merely coexist with Christianity: it does not really touch them, because it does not correspond to any real need. Only the presence of death will eventually produce in them the conditions under which they become fit for Christianity. The case of the Good Thief on the cross is typical: when everyone else, even the Apostles, had abandoned Christ, the thief became His disciple, because at that time he alone had the proper disposition of consciousness of sin.

But if each man must engender within himself the right

conditions for grace, it follows that grace has been made possible by a human disposition. How are we to reconcile this
with the notion of the complete rupture existing between
God and man? As we have already noted in the second chapter, Kierkegaard's ethical orientation tends very strongly to
emphasize the part played by the free will, so that in his
theory of sin he is forced constantly to guard against Pelagianism. Here we meet the same tendency. The aspect of human
freedom in the preparation for grace is so distinctly affirmed
that we cannot but conclude to the existence of a true syn-
ergistic theory of grace. God offers His justification first in
the revelation of sin, and man accepts it in the free admission
that he has a need for justification.[23] This synergism is by no
means restricted to the initial stage of grace; as we shall see
later, it plays a role throughout the development of the act of
faith. But in a certain sense all the necessary activity has
already been attained at this point, because man cannot do
more than need God. The need for God is man's highest perfection and his only intervention in the process of redemption. Christ will provide all the rest, but this one element
man must supply in full sincerity: the constantly renewed
need for God. The only means for achieving this is an increasingly interiorized consciousness of sin.

Up to this point Kierkegaard's presentation of Christianity
has seemed rather pessimistic. It is as if there exists an opportunity for faith only when all other vital sources have been
dried up (VIII A 47), and one is closest to despair. But, in
fact, faith is harsh only in order to create the opportunity for
redemption. Even if the revelation of sin paints a gloomy pic-

---

[23] The German Kierkegaard scholar E. Hirsch concludes, from an
examination of the idea of total guilt before God, that man's desire
and need for God at an earlier stage in the dialectic are, in themselves,
forms of grace (*op. cit.,* p. 859). In this case, we would be concerned
with a *gratia praeparans*. But even to this grace man must respond, and
Hirsch also speaks of synergism in this context (p. 899).

ture of man, this image is still more sanguine than that of paganism because of the perspective of salvation. The redemption does not, however, result in a new sort of "humanism," because grace has its origin *in* the very humiliation of man, and not *after*. It is in the consciousness of sin itself that God's grace comes to him. As soon, therefore, as a person feels profoundly guilty before God, he has already left sin behind. In the dialectical relation between God and man, the ultimate depth of rejection is also the beginning of salvation: out of repentance there arises the upward movement through which God's transcendency justifies man. *Consciousness of sin and forgiveness of sin* evoke each other with the internal necessity of two dialectical moments. But this dialectical necessity does not owe its origin to the immanent structure of reality, as in Hegel, but rather to God's absolutely free and redemptive intervention.[24] Between those two moments, which occur simultaneously in time, there yawns the same abyss as between God's all-holiness and human sinfulness. In spite of the presence of grace (which alone makes it possible for man to regard himself as a sinner), the whole consciousness of sin remains immersed in sinfulness. It is only in the forgiveness of sin that God's transcendency completely breaks through this barrier of sinfulness. This happens in the *instant*.

The *instant* is brought about by the synthesis of time and eternity (CD IV 391 LO 76). We already noted that the spirit can posit itself only in the acceptance or rejection of its transcendental origin, in the *possibility of sin*. As long as there is no possibility of sin, there exists neither spirit nor eternity; time and eternity remain confusedly united in an untemporal but also uneternal consciousness. But when man

[24] In the commentaries of J. Wahl, who has been strongly influenced by Hegel, it is rather difficult to discern the distinction between those two entirely different types of causes.

takes a definitive stand with respect to his own spiritual origin, he posits himself as spirit. Through sin man opted for the temporal, at the expense of the eternal: existence cut itself off from eternity. Thenceforth, temporality is essentially opposed to eternity, and, of itself, impotent to rediscover eternity. Christ's Incarnation restores the eternal dimension to the spirit and *reveals* man's intrinsic relation to an eternal Origin.[25] In the Incarnation eternity communicates itself personally to man's existence in time. It is *the* instant par excellence in which all temporality is integrated in Eternity. In the instant of the Incarnation Eternity comes into existence in time.

But by adopting a temporal existence, Eternity has bound Itself to a historical moment, the *fullness of time*. How, then, can a person living in a different historical epoch participate in this particular instant? Exactly when does the instant occur for him? The answer is: as soon as, by a profound faith that his sins have been forgiven him, he becomes a *contemporary* of Christ in his private life. In this faith the Incarnation becomes present for him, Eternity breaks through his temporality, and he opens himself to the approach of grace. In the *instant* time is transformed by God's eternity; this happened first in "the fullness of time" when Christ entered into human history, and it occurs once again in the personal act of faith in Christ.[26] In a first moment of faith in Christ, Eternity breaks through time and declares the whole of temporality to be sinful. Then, in a second moment (distinct, not tem-

[25] Wahl, *op. cit.*, p. 324, concludes from this that God's historical appearance presupposed sin, and therefore that the *redemption is the real cause of sin*. But his conclusion is correct only in a Hegelian dialectic where everything happens by immanent necessity. For Kierkegaard, however, between the factual situation of sin and the Incarnation lies the whole freedom of God's transcendent intervention.

[26] See also V. Lindström, "La Théologie de l'imitation de Jésus-Christ chez Søren Kierkegaard," *Revue d'Histoire et de Philosophie religieuses*, 35 (1955), p. 380.

porally, but purely dialectically, from the first), this sinfulness is removed and forgiven by eternity.

As was pointed out in the second chapter, Kierkegaard
regards the instant not as an element peculiar to Christianity,
but as a central element in every type of religion. The religious life on a sheerly natural basis, the so-called religiousness
A,[27] culminates in the consciousness of guilt before God. In
this affirmation of oneself before God, natural religion arrives
at an instant in which eternity touches existence in time,
but without penetrating it.[28] By a free admission of his guilt
man affirms his intrinsic relation with God and thus brings
something absolute into his existence. For this leap into the
absolute no direct intervention of God is required. The
instant of religiousness A has nothing to do with grace: time
and eternity remain irreconcilably opposed. The individual
feels himself to be essentially guilty, and to be averted from a

[27] As opposed to religiousness B which is based on revelation. Kierkegaard's natural religion has, of course, nothing to do with the seven-
teenth-century idea of *natura pura*—it deals with the concrete, the
sinful man who, nevertheless, does not know Christianity.

[28] The reader may raise the objection that, before this moment, the
spirit has already constituted itself as spirit in the commission of sin,
as Kierkegaard explicitly declares in *The Concept of Dread*. Yes, but
sin becomes sin only when it becomes sin *in the presence of*, or *before*,
God, and that occurs only in the consciousness of sin. In this sense, one
can say that sin becomes true *sin* only when it is no longer actual sin;
this is in accord with *The Sickness unto Death* (cf. Chapter 2, section
3). It is at the instant when the individual comes before God that he
becomes *sinner* (and so will have to choose again between faith and
despair). Consequently, it would be erroneous to conclude from *The
Concept of Dread* that man has become spirit through the simple commission of a moral transgression. Only at the moment when he sees his
faults *before God* does he become spirit. Here it should also be added
that, as the same Chapter 2, section 3 indicates, only a Christian can
be a *sinner before God*, in the full meaning of the expression, because
in his case alone does the consciousness of *guilt* become a genuine
consciousness of sin. From this it also follows that only the Christian
is able fully to become *spirit*.

God with Whom he must nevertheless continue to maintain a real relation: the proportion remains a disproportion.

The Christian, too, in his dialectic of interiorization, meets the same opposition, but for him it is not final: God Himself has sublated it by uniting time and eternity in His Incarnation. A Christian is able to believe in redemption, for he knows that God Himself has adopted our sinful temporality in His eternity. He alone, therefore, fully exists in the instant. Whenever an individual places himself *in the presence of God* with the consciousness of his guilt, he may be said to be existing in the instant; however, this notion finds its fullest expression only in Christianity, where Eternity Itself penetrates temporality.

At the point at which the instant attains to its fullness from faith in Christ, man begins a new existence, guided by the certitude that God, in the person of Christ, has forgiven him his sins. The forgiveness of sin is the great renewal that Christianity has brought forth in the world.

"Thy sins are forgiven thee" (Luke 7, 49), that is the cry of encouragement of the Christians to one another; with this cry Christianity spreads all over the world, by these words it is recognized a race apart, a separate nation (VIII A 644).[29]

The forgiveness of sin is a "transubstantiation" of reality; it creates a break between the present and all one's past life (III A 211).

[29] This forgiveness of sin cannot be overemphasized. Kierkegaard prefers the translation of Ezechiel 33, 16 in *The Imitation of Christ*— "None of his sins *shall enter into His mind*"—to the usual "shall he remember" or "shall be imputed to him," because the first sounds more forceful (X^2 A 283) (1018) [our translation].

4. Grace as Faith

This new life consists not in a rebirth to another nature, but in a new relationship with God, a novelty of faith.

The necessary condition for our salvation is *to believe* that everywhere and at all times there is an absolute beginning. . . . It is this infinite intensity in the *anticipation of faith* which has the courage to dare to believe, to dare to transform the past into absolute oblivion . . . and thenceforth to believe in an absolute beginning (X² A 371) [Italics ours].[30]

The relationship with God always remains dialectical, for, although the redemption is a *reality*, it is so transcendent that, even though it is adapted to human nature, it will never become entirely integrated therewith. It therefore will always be a reality *of faith*. The remission of sin is just as dialectical as the relationship with God, of which it constitutes a moment (IX A 482). God remains God and man remains man; the whole relation lies in the dialectical tension between sinfulness and forgiveness. Without the antithesis of sinfulness, forgiveness is unthinkable. At every moment the Christian is *simultaneously* sinner and justified: *simul justus et peccator*. Throughout all eternity we shall continue to be aware of the presence of our sins, and yet we shall be justified in Christ. Far from destroying each other, these two moments remain dialectically complementary. In their very opposition is to be found their reconciliation; the justification is never

[30] The phrase ἄφεσις τῶν παραπτωμάτων, as Kierkegaard observed as early as 1834, seems to mean not so much *forgiveness* of sins as it does *relaxation* of sin: through justification, man is placed in the proper *relationship,* so that the relation with sin is abolished, while the sins themselves remain (I A 6). But this text dates from a period when Kierkegaard had not yet stated the problem of the remission of sin with complete precision.

a static datum, once and for all, but always a dialectical process—one *is* justified only insofar as one *becomes* justified.

In this theory Kierkegaard has, after his own fashion, expressed a fundamental thesis of the Reformation. Christ is at every moment both our Judge and our Redeemer (X¹ A 29). In one and the same act of faith the Christian recognizes himself as sinner and as redeemed. This idea is to be found very early in Kierkegaard's writings:

That is really profound in Christianity: Christ is both our Savior and our Judge, not that there is one savior and one judge, for then we should certainly be sentenced, but that the Savior and the Judge are one (II A 261) (222).

The two opposite moments come together in the act of faith. Faith is the focal point where man receives God's forgiveness in his sinfulness. As the meeting point of God and man, faith is at once divine grace and the highest human activity.[31]

In faith, God's *grace* covers our *sinfulness* at every instant. Should either grace or sinfulness be removed, the dialectic is interrupted, and so, consequently, is the process of justification. In the religious relationship, therefore, false over-familiarity and an exaggerated feeling of remoteness are equally pernicious. Both deviations cause man to relapse into immanence—in the second, he considers his guilt to be more important than God's transcendency, and thus in a negative way subordinates it to himself. Only the *simul justus et peccator* attitude maintains God's transcendency, however shocking it may be to reason (IX A 427).

Because of this opposition, which it must continually bridge, faith in redemption, far from lessening the burden of

---

[31] The special structure of the act of faith will be studied in the next chapter; here we are considering this act only as the "outstretched hand" which receives God's grace.

man's conscience, creates an even greater tension than did the consciousness of sin.

To believe is exactly to lighten oneself by means of a considerable weight with which one burdens oneself. . . . It is like flying—but here one flies precisely because of the inverse reaction of a weight; a considerable weight is necessary in order to be light enough to be able to fly (VII A 177).

Justification lies outside the scope of all experience and is an object exclusively of faith. If it is true that sinfulness remains (though now *within* forgiveness), then a fortiori all its consequences, such as suffering and internal uncertainty, also remain. Not the punishment, but only that which makes the punishment unbearable, the consciousness of living in strife with God, is remitted (X^1 A 462). But this remission totally alters the punishment: henceforth, man knows that he is no longer living under a sentence of God's wrath (X^3 A 319; also earlier, II A 63 [116]).

Though redemption does not efface our sinful past (the *corpus peccati* of St. Paul), and though forgiveness of sin is not an object of experience, it does not fail to exert a strong influence on our daily life. Faith in the remission of sin is like a light that beckons, and gives the traveler the *courage* to retrace his steps (II A 63) (116).

It is simply that the transgression is *pardoned,* the remission of sin is nothing more. It is not a matter of becoming another man under happier circumstances, but of becoming a new man in the comforting realization that the sin is pardoned, even if the consequences of the transgression remain. . . . It is only he who understands that sin is entirely different from, and dreadful in quite another way than, the consequences of the transgression (such as unhappiness, suffering, etc.), it is only he who repents . . . (VII A 141).

Kierkegaard points out explicitly that, as Luther remarks, Christ is Redeemer not for this but for the eternal life.[32] In this doctrine lies all the difference between the Jewish and the Christian religion. Judaism makes promises only for this life (X^3 A 138). "Its slogan is to keep on God's side, so that all may go well in life" (X^3 A 139). For a Christian, on the contrary, the new life remains essentially a promise for the future. In this world man will always bear the stigma of sin. He possesses the certainty of forgiveness but not the triumph of redemption; the latter is reserved for the hereafter.

What, then, has redemption accomplished? It re-establishes the dialogue with God. By *putting on Christ*, man can once again appear before God. One should conceive of this "putting on" as more than an exterior imputation; however, it never becomes identity with oneself.

In speaking of Christ, one does not say: seek to resemble Him, (for to speak in this way indirectly implies that two still remain essentially dissimilar), no, but: put Him on, yes, put Him on—as when one wears rented clothing (which is the *satisfactio vicaria*), put Him on—as when someone's double seeks not simply to resemble him but to "impersonate" him. Christ gives you His clothing (*satisfactio*) and then requires that you "impersonate" Him (X^2 A 255).

Ultimately, the novelty of Christian existence appears to be a novelty of *faith*, in which man puts his entire salvation in Christ's hands and trusts that in Him all his sins will be forgiven. In this supreme act of trust he vanishes in Christ. It is no longer his sinfulness, but Christ's justice, which appears in the sight of God; and under this aspect the believer, without any merit of his own, is "declared" righteous in Christ. As much as Kierkegaard combats the notion of a

[32] This statement applies only to the consequences of sin, sinfulness, and not to sin itself, as we shall have occasion to see further on.

triumph of the redemption in the present, he insists that the *forgiveness* of sin was not promised for the world to come, for eternity, but takes place in time, in the present.[33] Otherwise we could only trust that God's love would remit the punishment for our sins in the hereafter (VIII A 649) (753). But such an expectation is not faith in the *forgiveness of sin* itself. Forgiveness must take place in this life, while man is still in the situation of sin. In the afterlife only the effects of sin will be in question. The true forgiveness of sins—and this is what the priest means when he says, "I forgive you your sins" in the present—is a new creation in this world (VII A 78) (581).

The new life of faith implies not only God's grace but the highest human activity as well. Redemption is not an external *gift* which envelops man without affecting him interiorly, but a God-given *task* which puts his intellectual and volitional life to the decisive ordeal of becoming spirit. Once man has come to realize what it means to be sinful not just in one or another particular matter, but in every way, in his existence itself, faith in the redemption becomes a very difficult challenge. Unless he meets this challenge, eternity will never break through his temporality—and he will never fully become spirit. Only a living faith in God's redemption can revitalize the past in the present and recall man from fleeting time. Faith is the *instant* in which eternity penetrates into time and makes man into spirit.

That man, then, who has truly lived and does live the ordeal of believing in the forgiveness of his sins—that man has certainly become another man. . . . Belief in the forgiveness of his sins is the decisive crisis through which a man becomes spirit; he who does not believe in this is not spirit (VIII A 673).

[33] It is noteworthy that Kierkegaard finds as an adversary here the same Mynster whom he also opposed because of the latter's theory of triumphant Christianity, which held that the fullness of redemption took place in this world (X² A 75; cf. *supra,* p. 150).

Faith is at once *act* and *gift*. The act of faith is a leap into the void, a total surrender to God in which man abandons any foothold and in an ultimate choice realizes his freedom. On the other hand, this "choice" is specified by an object which, as completely transcendent, lies beyond all choice. Because of its transcendent object, the *act* of faith is intrinsically transformed and elevated to a supernatural order. God communicates with man within the framework of his own activity.

To posit the act of faith man must be provided with the necessary condition—entirely beyond his reach (PF IV 208-9 LO 10). The *objective* precondition of Christ's Incarnation is not sufficient. God must also intervene in the subjective appropriation of this objective redemption, for the object of faith always remains transcendent and outside the human grasp. It never becomes an objective gift, the appropriation of which is simply left up to everyone's personal powers. The act of faith, therefore, is a result of freedom and grace together.

Thus, the will to believe must itself be induced by God. In a more intellectual fashion, Kierkegaard traces, in his *Philosophical Fragments*, the development of this all-pervasive working of God's grace. In reply to the question posed in Plato's *Meno* as to whether truth can be taught, Kierkegaard makes a distinction between an immanent truth that is to be found within the pupil himself, rendering the teacher's work superfluous (the Socratic method), and a transcendent truth for which the teacher must continually provide the very conditions for understanding. If a truth is really transcendent, the pupil can never understand it unless the teacher remolds his mind (PF IV 208-09 LO 9-10). Christianity is such a truth; unlike a philosophical system that is established once and for all, the object of faith must be fashioned anew within each individual. As with Jesus' contemporaries, God Himself must furnish us with the conditions for belief. It is impossible to receive the teachings of Christianity at second hand. "Thus faith must steadily hold fast to the teacher" (PF IV 254 LO 50). To consider Christianity as an objective truth which everyone can appropriate to himself is to miss its very essence, for God alone can teach man anything about Himself. When Christianity becomes a "doctrine," it becomes detached from God and petrified: it is no longer a divine message.

It would be wrong to confine Kierkegaard's theology of grace, even in the rather intellectualist *Philosophical Fragments,* to an appropriation of transcendent *truth.* The concept of "condition for faith" implies something much richer than pure *understanding.* Just as faith is not restricted to an act of the intellect (PF IV 254 LO 50), but involves the whole man, so the condition on which faith depends transforms man in his totality. Christ is not just the Teacher, but also the Redeemer, that is, the Creator of new life in which it becomes possible to hear God's word of forgiveness.[34] Grace, then, may be defined as the necessary condition for a new relationship with God, a condition which at once precedes, and coincides with, the relationship itself.

Faith and grace presuppose one another. Without faith there would be no grace, because Incarnation and Redemption become realities only in faith. Without grace, on the other hand, no faith is possible, because faith transcends all human possibilities.

Faith posits something prior to itself which otherwise would not exist (grace). But it posits it as *prior to itself* and so acknowledges that it exists entirely independently. As seen from without, faith is for the first time creating the new world of God, whereas, as

---

[34] This new creation is not to be understood in the Catholic sense of that term, but as a novelty of faith through which man, despite his sinfulness, establishes himself in a new relationship with God.

JUDGMENT AND GRACE103

considered from within, faith is merely building further on the
eternal ground of God.[35]

Faith commits itself so completely to God that it recognizes
God as the source of its very existence (X^3 A 298) (1123). The
activity of the human will in faith becomes possible only
through a choice by God Himself: only *within* the limits of
the *datum* of grace, which transcends all freedom, can faith
be called free.

It is easy to see . . . that faith is not [merely] an act of will; for all
human volition has its capacity within this scope of an underlying
condition. . . . If I do not have the condition . . . all my willing
is of no avail (PF IV 255 LO 50-51).

Thus human activity remains unrestricted in faith, but it
takes place within the framework of a grace, which remains
exclusively God's. It is to this operation of grace that Kierkegaard is referring in the pseudonymous works of his first
period when he speaks of faith as an act of willing *by virtue
of the absurd.*
Faith is a transition between contrition and forgiveness of
sin. Contrition, taken in itself, would be possible without
grace. The remission of sin, which comes later, is entirely
grace. But faith, which comprehends both the consciousness
of sin and the certainty of remission, lies between the two as
a union of free will and grace. This is not to say, however, that
in contrition, *as preparation for faith*, grace is not yet at
work! In fact, consciousness of sin as opposed to consciousness
of guilt is a datum of revelation and the first moment of justification itself. In a Christian perspective contrition is to be
found just outside the moment of faith and, as a *predisposi-
tion* for faith, participates by anticipation in the grace of

[35] Thust, *op. cit.*, p. 355. For clarity's sake, we have translated *Voraus-
setzung* as *faith*, which is what it really means in this context.

faith. In the dialectic of faith each of the various moments receives its final determination from the whole: therefore, contrition has an entirely different meaning for someone who has become justified in faith than for the nonbeliever.

If faith were not, from its very inception, grace, man by his own power would create within himself a disposition which would necessitate grace. Thus man himself would effect his salvation, and the whole process of justification would ultimately depend on human effort. In spite of his emphasis on the necessity of man's free co-operation,[36] Kierkegaard firmly maintains that each step preparatory to the reception of God's grace must itself already be grace.

The modern Christian exhibits a strong tendency to over-estimate his alleged role in the process of justification. (In return, however, he will forget about the real demands.) He has forgotten that grace is, first and foremost, *forgiveness of sins*, about which man can do nothing but surrender himself unconditionally to God.

The Penitent Woman of the Gospel realized that she could contribute nothing to her forgiveness save the acceptance of her incapacity. She did not wait until she felt worthy to go to the house of the Savior, because in that case she would never have gone. And when she did go, it was as if she were going to a great feast, for she knew that no amount of self-torture could bring her closer to salvation. And so, almost frivolously, she took with her only what was proper to a feast—fragrant balm. In Jesus' presence she did not grope for well-chosen words—she was silent, and wept. And her tears flowed only because she could not restrain them. The only thing to which she contributed was the feast, because she clearly saw that she could do nothing toward the remission of her sins: she anointed Jesus' feet with her balm, and

[36] In the next section we will see again how this distinguishes him from most theologians of the Reformation.

dried them with her hair. She did not even hear what others were muttering about her, because all that was of no consequence to her. She heard only one thing: Many sins have been forgiven her. But then the Master added: "Because she has loved much." And Kierkegaard concludes:

I assume that this last word she did not hear at all; it perhaps might have troubled her that there was a "because" and as applied to her it might perhaps have alarmed love to hear itself praised thus. Hence I assume that she did not hear it, or perhaps she heard it but heard amiss so that she thought He said, "because He loved much" so that what was said had reference to His infinite love, that because it was so infinite, therefore her many sins were forgiven her! (DC XII 303 LO 268).

Whoever is able to evaluate his true condition will realize that there is no room left for any "initiative" on man's part. Man is not able to convert a negative relation with God into a positive one (TC XII 24-33 LO 11-20). God Himself must *draw* man unto Himself. Kierkegaard elaborates on this idea in *Training in Christianity* apropos of John 12, 32: "And I, if I be lifted up from the earth, will draw all unto Me." Only Christ can draw me toward eternity. To believe is to be drawn by Christ—it is the free renunciation of all active achievement, the admission of one's inability to eradicate guilt (III C 16). Therefore, faith justifies only insofar as it abandons all justification.

This is also what Christ taught us in the Parable of the Pharisee and the Publican. The pharisee attempted to justify himself, but instead returned home with a new sin, heavier than all the previous ones; the publican accused himself and went home justified.

Before God to wish to justify oneself, that precisely is to denounce oneself as guilty; but before God to smite oneself upon the breast,

saying, "God be merciful to me a sinner" that precisely is to
justify oneself, or rather it is the condition for God's pronouncing
thee justified (HP XI 299 LO 396).

The basic element in the act of faith is man's recognition
of his complete impotence. The man of faith acknowledges
his own irreparable injustice and in his heart finds only self-
condemnation, but he believes that God is greater than his
heart (CD X 347-54 LO 297-303; the text comes from 1 John
3, 20). Without this attitude man cannot be reached by God's
grace. For only a humble admission of impotence and a
strong belief in God despite this impotence is able to preserve
the transcendence of grace.[37]

It should be obvious that sacraments in the Catholic, or
even in the orthodox Lutheran, sense of the word are in-
compatible with Kierkegaard's theory. He accepts baptism
and communion, but only as tokens of faith.[38] In his earlier
writings he even raises objections against the baptism of
infants, because the act of faith is strictly personal and cannot
be presumed from the faith of the parents. Later he accepts
infant baptism, as the anticipation of the *possibility* of becoming a Christian, but in no case can baptism be considered
any longer as "the decisive criterion" for being a Christian
(PS VII 601 LO 539).

As time went on, Kierkegaard's dislike for the usual notion
of the sacraments grew more intense. In his posthumous
papers we find the following comment:

It is because of the place we have assigned to the sacraments, and
the use we have made of them, that Christianity has been reduced

[37] In this theory Kierkegaard carries the *sola fide* doctrine to its most
extreme point, regardless of what his other teachings concerning the
opera fidei may be. Cf. L. Chestov, *Kierkegaard et la philosophie existentielle* (Paris, 1948), p. 361.

[38] About the Eucharist as "token of the reception of the Lord," cf. ED
XII 335.

to Judaism. And it is very true—probably the truest statement about Christendom—that, as Pascal says, it is a union of people who, by means of the sacraments, excuse themselves from their duty to love God. By baptism we become objectively part of God's people, and even by baptism at infancy—just as one becomes one of God's people through circumcision (XI A 556).[39]

5. Grace as Freedom

Once having clearly established God's initiative, one should not fear to give full weight to man's active response. Grace, after all, constitutes a relationship, and a relationship cannot exist without two *real* terms. Only God can bring about this relationship, but even He is powerless if man, the other term involved, does not choose with all his force to accept God's causal activity. By excluding human freedom the predestination theory in effect destroys the second term and, with it, the relationship itself.

From every point of view the concept predestination may be considered as an abortion, for having unquestionably arisen in order to relate freedom and God's omnipotence, it solves the riddle by

[39] On this point, one may consult Geismar, S. *Kierkegaard* (Goettingen, 1929), pp. 593-94. Taken only literally, of course, the quoted passage simply constitutes a warning against objectivism and exteriorization, but behind it lies Kierkegaard's idea of the subjective realization of Christianity, which is necessarily antagonistic to all sacramental objectivizing. With W. Ruttenbeck, we agree that anything in Kierkegaard's writings in the area of sacramentology that points in the direction of Catholicism is to be considered as a deviation from his basic views on this matter *Søren Kierkegaard, Der Christliche Denker und sein Werk* (Berlin, 1929), (p. 236). However, we would not broaden this critical conclusion to include Kierkegaard's comments on authority: what he has to say about the latter is sufficiently comprehensible within his doctrine of subjectivity, because authority itself must be understood dialectically. Cf. Chapter VI of this book.

denying one of the concepts and consequently explains nothing
(I A 5) (2).

In the predestinationist interpretation grace becomes a
neutral object, instead of a relation between two free agents.
The theory of predestination attempts to reconcile the concept of freedom with the idea of Divine Providence. But it
solves nothing, for what was to have been the solution has
now become a new problem (I A 7). It results from a rationalistic theology, which refutes itself by its own conclusion (III
A 31).[40]

In his later years Kierkegaard tried to justify his initial
dislike for the theory of predestination by means of his own
philosophy: predestination disregards the subjectivity which
is the very source of religion.

In order to overcome subjectivity they maintain, correctly, that
no one is saved by his own works, but by grace—and, corresponding to grace, by faith.

All right. But can I myself do nothing, then, to become a believer? Here, it is necessary either to answer immediately with an
unqualified no, and then we have election to grace in the fatalistic sense, or else to make a slight concession. The fact is that one
has always been distrustful of the subjective, and in establishing
the principle of salvation by faith one immediately suspected that
just this in itself was conceding too much. So one immediately
adds: but of himself, no one can give himself grace—it is a gift
of God that must be obtained by prayer.

All right; but can I, then, pray by my own power, or must we
go further and say: No, praying (and so also praying in order to
have faith) is a gift of God that no one can give himself—it is

---

[40] It is to be observed that all the texts quoted date from Kierkegaard's
early period. (He was in his twenty-second year when he wrote I A 5 and
I A 7.) This may explain somewhat the great ease with which he dis-
poses of the problem.

necessary that we be given it. And then what? Then it is certainly
necessary, in turn, that it be given me to pray in a suitable manner
to obtain faith, etc. There we have a case of envelope containing
envelope . . . but at some moment it is necessary to come to a halt
at subjectivity. To extend the ladder to so great a length and to
make the climb so difficult is perhaps a praiseworthy means of
expressing, as His majesty requires, God's infinity; but to exclude
subjectivity is, just the same, not feasible, unless one wants fatal-
ism (X^2 A 301).

But Kierkegaard also senses the opposite danger of Semi-
Pelagianism, which limits God's role to the external revelation of an object of faith, that man, entirely by his own
choice, integrates into his personal life. This doctrine undermines the gratuitousness, and consequently also the transcendency, of grace.

All the initiative rests with God: that is the element of
truth in the predestination theory. Hence it follows that man
is totally dependent on His omnipotence. But God's omnipotence is love. Love gives itself, and omnipotent love can give
itself in such a way that, in the very giving, it withdraws and
makes a being free to become itself. We human beings can
never make any creature free, for we are bound to the very
power by which we create and thus immediately bring the
being that we wanted to liberate into a relationship of dependence (VII A 181). God is not bound to the power by
which He created us: He is supremely free. That is why His
creatures can be free. In fact we are so completely free that
we are able to turn away from the source of our freedom.

Predestinationism entirely neglects this element of freedom and, as a result, ends up with a fatalistic theory of salvation. The main problem, from a human viewpoint, is not
whether one has been elected, but whether one is going to
respond to God's election.

People argue whether God wishes the salvation of all or only of some—they almost forget the so much more important consideration: Thou, O God! Who willest my salvation, may I also be able to will it! (X¹ A 516).

Only a distinction between two simultaneous operations, that of the Holy Ghost and that of man himself, in the acceptance of grace, makes it possible to steer between Semi-Pelagianism and predestinationism (I A 37).

For his justification man depends entirely on God, in Whom alone rests the power to sanctify him. But within the limits of this dependence, man is totally free, so that he can either co-operate with God or undo His plan of salvation. God's initiative brings about the possibility of a new relation, but without man's co-operation it will never become a *real* relation (X¹ A 59). Still, this does not mean that God and man are to each other as equal partners: man's freedom is effective only within his total dependence.

It is as when one gives a present to a child and then, to please him, pretends that he is giving us what we have given him, which in fact was ours. But our relationship with God is not even of that kind, for God is also at the same time the One Who gives us the power to succeed. It would, therefore, be like the father and mother who themselves help the child to write a congratulatory letter for their anniversary, which letter will be received as a present on the anniversary day (VIII A 342).

In the process of redemption the Christian uses his freedom only to assent to what he has received. And this includes everything, for everything that comes from God is grace. The whole structure of events by which life continues in its course, and which the pagan calls fate, is part of what has been *given* by God—and given for our salvation. Providence, in fact, becomes part of the redemption, for the redemption is nothing but the continuation of God's love for man after sin. In Christ, God's plan for man has acquired a new meaning.

The redemption is the continued providence that God will care for the individual and for what is most individual in him in spite of the fact that he has lost everything (VII A 130) (602).

It is up to us to discover in our lives God's design. This is far from easy, for we often have the feeling that the circumstances of our lives are a matter of blind fate, irreconcilable with the idea of an all-loving God. And so, many a Christian reading the words of St. James 1, 17, "Every good and perfect gift is from above, coming down from the Father of lights, with whom there is no change, nor shadow of alteration," will think to himself:

This saying sounds to my ears almost like a cruelty, for my lot has been nothing but suffering and misery; of course I cannot deny that the saying is true, that every perfect gift comes down from above, I can only say that for me it has not come down (X¹ A 292).

Then man begins to question God about his lot. And when God does not answer his question, it becomes a cry of distress: Is God Himself subject to fate? If this desperate protest does not cut man off from God altogether, it is the most profound acknowledgment of His transcendency. Like Job the believer feels that before God he is always wrong, even if he is right, because God is God and towers above all human notions of right (R III 272 LO 129-30).

Only when a person has risen to the relationship of love with God, can suffering become a *trial*. In the state of sin suffering merely expressed the infinite distance of which the individual was conscious; but when a man suffers and at the same time must still be confident that God loves him, his pain causes an almost unbearable tension. Worse than all suffering is the idea that God's love manifests itself in this suffering, that *this* is His grace and that He has nothing better to offer us.

Humanly speaking, Job's wife was, in a sense, right. For oh, really is it not, humanly, a tremendous extra burden, when one is suffering so much, to have to torment oneself in addition with the idea that, despite everything, God is love. That is something to lose one's mind on—and, humanly speaking, it is so much easier to despair without further ado (X[1] A 478) (930).

Grace itself puts faith to the most severe test: no worse crisis is possible than having to accept the thought that *through suffering* God is showing his love. In this supreme tension of the trial, faith can only reject all "proofs" of God's love and cling blindly to God's own word that He is faithful forever. Amid the despair of this world appears the triumph of faith; freed from all other ties, it adheres exclusively to the Redeemer Himself. Nothing remains but the certitude of faith: "I know that my Redeemer liveth!" For the true believer this certitude is sufficient to transform the greatest of adversities into a blessing (VIII A 509). In such a frame of mind Kierkegaard wrote the following prayer:

O loving Father, nothing succeeds for me—and yet Thou art love. Alas! I fail in this too: to maintain steadfastly that Thou art love and yet Thou art. Wherever I turn, the one thing that I cannot escape and that cannot be gainsaid is that Thou art love; and that is why, when I fail to maintain that Thou art love, yet I believe that it is Thy love which allows this failure. O infinite love! (X[3] A 49).

In the trial, faith is freed of its last connections with *things*, to become purely a relationship to a *Person*. My sinfulness no longer interferes with my salvation, for my sin is mine, whereas my certitude is God's (VII A 130) (602). Such certainty would be presumption if it had originated in myself, but I only adhere to it because God commands it. Only at God's command does man dare to be sure of his justification.[41] That is why his certainty is firm as rock, and why, ultimately, faith is absolute obedience.

The believer, therefore, is the man of character, who, in absolute obedience to God, regards it as a duty not to want to understand (X[1] A 367).

Nowhere does God's absolute primacy manifest itself more clearly in the process of justification than in this demand of obedience. It is important to emphasize this before analyzing the notions of faith and imitation of Christ, in which Kierkegaard stresses the activity of man so much. Faith always remains a task assigned from above, in which man has no initiative. It is God who leads; man's role is unconditional obedience.

[41] "You must believe: there is the eternally consoling basis of the doctrine of the remission of sins. For when the anguished conscience has begun to think sad thoughts and it seems that one for all eternity cannot forget, then resound the words: you must forget, you must not ruminate upon your sins—not just, 'You may,' not just, 'You dare ask God permission to dare forget,' but, 'You must forget,' because you must believe that your sin is forgiven you" (IX A 177).

IV

THE DIALECTIC OF THE ACT OF FAITH

1. *Objectivity and Subjectivity*

KIERKEGAARD'S THEORY of faith must be understood as a reaction against Hegel. For Hegel, faith is primarily an undeveloped form of knowledge:

What I believe, that I also know; it is content in my consciousness; faith is a knowledge, but by knowledge one usually understands a mediated cognition.[1]

The whole of rational thought is already present in faith, but not in the form of science; it is there only as *representation*. Faith, therefore, is an immediate stage of thought, the content of which must be made explicit by reflection and ultimately be developed into science.[2]

Initially, Kierkegaard knew the Hegelian position only

---

[1] G. W. F. Hegel, *Philosophie der Religion* (Jubiläumausg.), pp. 129-30. See also *Encyclopädie* (Lassonausg), p. 554.
[2] G. W. F. Hegel, *Phenomenology of Mind*, trans. by J. B. Baillie (London, 1949), pp. 549-58.

indirectly, through the lectures of H. N. Clausen and H. Martensen, and especially through Erdmann's *Vorlesungen über Glauben und Wissen*, with which he already had become acquainted in the year of its publication, 1837 (II C 38-49). For Erdmann, as for Hegel, faith is an imperfect form of knowledge: it receives its object from without. In order to become *truth*, the content of faith must first be produced by reason from within itself, by means of idealistic philosophy. Thus the dualism of the act of faith is terminated in the unity of the philosophic "notion."

Kierkegaard was never an idealist,[3] but his magistral thesis in theology unquestionably exhibits strong Hegelian influence.[4] Later he almost completely freed himself from this influence; nevertheless, many of his categories originated in reaction to Hegel—and thus show at least a negative influence.

In an unpublished paper, *Johannes Climacus*, composed early in 1843, Kierkegaard, in a manner strongly reminiscent of Hegel's *Phenomenology*, attempted to determine the stages of consciousness leading to faith (IV B 1). In a first moment consciousness is totally *immediate*, that is, indeterminate. Since there is nothing whatever of relation here, there is likewise no problem of truth: every impression as an immediate datum is "true," but must at the very next moment give way to a new datum, and thus it becomes untrue. The immediate, therefore, is not yet full consciousness, but only a moment in the process of consciousness. According to Hegel, full consciousness is reached when subject and object are united as two terms of one relationship, which he calls *reflection*. But for Kierkegaard, Hegel's reflection only creates the *possibility* for a relationship which, in order to become *real*, requires a

---

[3] This has already been shown by E. Hirsch, and recently in more detail by W. Anz, *Kierkegaard und der deutsche Idealismus*.

[4] See, for example, his own remarks X³ A 477; cf. also Anz, *op. cit.*

third element, a passionate interest of the subject in its object. As long as the subject has only a speculative interest in its object, the two terms remain aloof from each other and are not wholly united. The relationship, and consequently also consciousness, is not fully actualized in reflection. Reflection is "dichotomic," while full consciousness is "trichotomic."

This distinction is needed for an exact conception of faith and doubt. Both presuppose a personal involvement of the subject. Reflection is not yet a real relationship between subject and object and, consequently, is incapable of doubt and faith. Disinterested knowledge (aesthetics, mathematics or metaphysics) can be a condition of doubt, but the subject is too loosely connected with its object to create a real doubt.[5] Doubt is situated on a higher level than objective thought. However much subject and object in reflection may be opposed, doubt is not posited before there is conscious interest of the subject in this opposition. Similarly, with the disappearance of interest, doubt itself disappears. This insight was precisely that of the Greeks when they proposed *apathy* as the only resolution of doubt.

From this theory of consciousness it follows that no objective knowledge can ever sublate faith. In the act of faith we are infinitely interested, because it concerns our eternal salvation; whereas objective knowledge as such never appeals to our subjectivity. *True* (as opposed to *immediate*) faith is possible only *beyond* the stage of reflection, of objectivity. In the sphere of faith, arguments for the truth or the probability of faith are useless, for they belong to a lower level of con-

---

[5] By this distinction, Kierkegaard accepts a type of knowledge which precedes full *consciousness* and abandons Hegel's concept of consciousness. He also distinguishes the merely speculative uncertainty from the real, necessarily impassioned, doubt. He makes this distinction in a later text of his diary, which, despite long searching, I have been unable to relocate.

sciousness (cf. also V A 28). The characteristic of faith is commitment by the subject.

Just as inadequate as Hegel's objectivism would be a theory that defines faith as *sentiment*. From the beginning Kierkegaard reacted against Schleiermacher's view of religion as "feeling of dependency"; religious consciousness may originate as sentiment, but its true essence is reflective, or more properly, post-reflective. Religion begins where ordinary reflection ends. This means that faith "goes further" than philosophy, and not the opposite. As early as 1836—he was then twenty-three—Kierkegaard notes:

What Schleiermacher calls "Religion" and the Hegelians "Faith" is at the bottom only the first condition for everything—the vital fluidum—the atmosphere we breathe in—which does not really deserve this name (I A 273) (78).

Sentiment leads to religiosity, never to religion. He retained this position: in 1850 we still find him attacking Schleiermacher's sentiment of dependency on the ground that this theory deprives religion of its dialectical movement and makes it simply a static situation, a mere datum (X² A 417).

For Kierkegaard faith, like thought, is a dialectic of subject and object. But in faith the tension acquires infinite potentialities both because the subject is infinitely interested and because the object is not a pure datum of reason itself, and thus is not immediately assimilable by the mind. In faith there is no primordial identity between subject and object by which the objective data could compel reason to assent or to dissent; faith involves an acceptance of something not "given" by reason and never deducible from a previous content of consciousness. There is no continuity between consciousness of forgiveness and consciousness of sin, as there is between certainty and uncertainty. Subject and object are fundamentally opposed in faith, and the acceptance of its "data" is achieved in a dialectical process which goes deeper by far than pure reflection.

A faith which presents itself as *objectively* true is no faith at all for Kierkegaard. True, one sort of apologetics has tried to establish the truth of revelation in a way such that it would impose itself on all men and spare them the difficult dialectic of interiorization. But all such attempts are doomed to failure, for all the so-called "scientific proofs" of faith are based on the initial error that faith can be proved. Faith rests ultimately on free decision; thus it depends in the last analysis exclusively on subjectivity. No possible objectivity can ever relieve man of the responsibility to choose for himself.

Hence we do not here raise the question of the truth of Christianity in the sense that when this has been determined the subject is assumed ready and willing to accept it. No, the question is as to the mode of the subject's acceptance; and it must be regarded as an illusion . . . to assume that the transition from something objective to the subjective acceptance is a direct transition following upon the objective deliberation as a matter of course. On the contrary, the subjective acceptance is precisely the decisive factor; and an objective acceptance of Christianity (sit venia verbi) is paganism or thoughtlessness (PS VII 114-15 LO 115-16).

If Christianity is essentially subjectivity, it is a mistake for the observer to be objective. In every case where the object of knowledge is the very inwardness of the subjectivity of the individual, it is necessary for the knower to be in a corresponding position (PS VII 44 LO 51).

Therefore, every objective approach to Christianity is illegitimate; concerning faith, no speculation is possible except whether one accepts it or not. That is precisely the question. The Hegelian theologian, in trying to integrate Christianity as an objective datum in his system, in fact puts the real problem in parentheses.

Yet one also finds traces of such "objectivism" within the strictest orthodoxy. It concentrates by preference on the Bible, in hope of thereby giving the truth of faith an historical foundation. Members of this school attach utmost importance to scientific biblical study. Kierkegaard considers this work most useful; however, it has nothing to do with faith. Historical studies and textual criticism remain in essence approximative. But in matters of faith our eternal salvation is at stake. If our faith were based on an objectively correct text, the least variant would acquire capital importance, the smallest doubt about the authenticity of an inspired text would fill us with despair. At all times, we would be in a state of frenzied eagerness to devour, as quickly as possible, the most recently published work of Biblical exegesis. And we would very likely go to the grave with despair in our hearts, because the definitive study, on which the greatest scientists had collaborated, was not to appear until a few weeks later. And suppose, now, that we did not die, but instead lived to see this last, definitive study, so that not the least vestige of a problem remained concerning the Bible—what then? Would anyone who had no faith before, have come even a step closer to it? Not one! And he who had already been a believer, would he have gained anything? Nothing! On the contrary, it would be extremely dangerous for him, because he might then be inclined to confuse faith with science, if he should not hold himself in fear and trembling (PS VII 20 LO 30).

I assume now the opposite, that the opponents have succeeded in proving what they desire about the scriptures, with a certainty transcending the most ardent wish of the most passionate hostility

—what then? Have the opponents thereby abolished Christianity? By no means, not in the least. Has the opponent made good a right to be relieved of responsibility of not being a believer? Not in the least (PS VII 21 LO 31).

Whenever faith is concerned, objective certitude about the Bible can neither add nor detract anything. Besides, all the authority of the Bible derives from inspiration, but inspiration presupposes faith and cannot be deduced from the Bible even by the most powerful argument. Faith, then, is not to be founded on the Bible, the Bible is to be founded on faith.

To avoid the difficulties of the historical method inherent in an attempt to ground religion in the Bible, some Protestant thinkers took refuge in the notion of the Church. Grundtvig, to whom Kierkegaard assigns the dubious honor of this dis-covery, eliminates all historical arguments which are ap-proximate, by founding faith on a datum belonging not to the past but to the present: the Church. To demand further proofs here would be like asking a living man to prove his own existence. The objectivity of the undeniable fact of the existing Church is sufficient once and for all to safeguard one's faith.

On the contrary, Kierkegaard maintains, this argument merely postpones the difficulty, for the Church has authority only if it can prove that it is apostolic, that is the same as it was eighteen hundred years ago. We are back to the historical proof we have already rejected for the Bible. Consequently, this renewed effort to ground faith objectively turns out to have been in vain. The only way out is to accept faith as a primitive fact, irreducible to any objective datum.

Kierkegaard gives G. E. Lessing credit for pointing this out, by his repeated attacks against every form of objectively-founded Christianity. Lessing asks whether the historical facts of Christian religion, even supported by a plethora of scientific certainty, could provide a sufficient foundation on which to build one's eternal salvation. His answer is negative. Between these two there is a qualitative disproportion, irreducible from an objective viewpoint. However, from these premises Kierkegaard derives a conclusion different from that of the skeptic Lessing. If anyone is convinced that there is some reliability in the historical facts, he should act as Socrates did with respect to the soul's immortality. Socrates did not first go about collecting materials to support his point, and then live by faith in these proofs; he was absorbed so completely in the question itself that he did not hesitate to stake his life on it. Risking one's whole self is the only possible proof both for immortality and for the truth of the Christian religion (X² A 406) (1044). All others are insufficient.

All this world history and the reasons and proofs for the truth of Christianity must be suppressed. There is only one proof, one alone: that of faith. If I am really convinced (and that is a determination of interiority in the spiritual life), then for me my conviction is always superior to arguments; it is, strictly speaking, the conviction which provides the arguments and not the arguments, the conviction. . . .

I may possibly start with a motive, but this is the lowest stage. After that one makes one's choice. Under the weight of our responsibility before God, there originates a conviction which comes from God. At this point we are in the positive. This conviction can no longer be defended or proved by arguments, for the arguments are on a lower level. No, it becomes a personal question, a matter in which the whole person is staked. This conviction can only be defended by an ethical staking of oneself, i.e. by the sacrifices one is ready to bring to it, by the undauntedness with which it is maintained. There is only one argument for the truth of Christianity: the interior proof, the *argumentum Spiritus Sancti* (X A 481).

Thus Kierkegaard rejects any objective foundation of faith and replaces it by a "pathological proof" (in the etymological sense of pathos).

There is only one proof for the truth of Christianity, and that is precisely the pathological proof: when the anguish of sin and the pangs of his conscience force a man to cross the narrow dividing line which separates the despair bordering on madness and . . . Christianity. There lies Christianity (X[1] A 467).[6]

Here we have the Archimedean point for faith: pure interiority which, free from every objective datum, becomes capable of lifting this world by placing itself outside it (X[2] A 529).

Faith properly so called can never be alarmed by rational objections. Its attitude toward them is completely aprioristic. The believer knows that nothing in this world can separate him from Christ (II A 190). By a leap, faith takes man beyond all rational thought into a new world. In this sense, faith is immediate, but immediate in a way that can never be sublated by thought.

[6] Or, as Kierkegaard says in another entry of his diary: "What does he care for all the objections brought against Christianity, the man who is truly conscious of being a sinner, and truly experiences belief in the forgiveness of sins, and is saved in that name and in that faith from his former sins. There the only conceivable objection would be: but you might possibly have been saved in a different way. To that he cannot answer. It is as though one were to say to someone in love, yes, but you might have fallen in love with another girl; to which he would have to answer: There is no answer to that, for I only know that she is my love. The moment a lover can answer that objection he is *eo ipso* not in love. If a believer can answer that objection he is *eo ipso* not a believer" (X[1] A 443) (922).

2. *Subjectivity and Dialectic*

Now let us examine in greater detail the nature of this nonobjective faith. As a relation to God, faith has a spiritual character. This means, first of all, that the relation lies entirely within *subjectivity* which, for Kierkegaard, constitutes the *essence* of the spirit. The closer our relationship with God, the more we grow within, so that the whole religious life can be viewed as a process of interiorization. A second conclusion, resulting from the first, is that our relationship with God is necessarily dialectical. The spirit cannot grasp its own essence (subjectivity) without continually objectifying itself; but since the resulting objectivity is not proper to the essence of spirit, spirit must always leave it again to turn back to itself. Objectivity, then, is a necessary pole for the ascent of the spirit. Spirit uses objectivity as the rungs of a ladder to which one clings and from which one loosens one's grasp to pull oneself up.

As to the first of these characteristics of faith, subjectivity, Kierkegaard concludes that the degree of involvement of the subject increases to the extent that objective certainty diminishes. Subjective interest in the act of faith reaches its peak when every shred of objective certainty disappears.

We have seen that faith withdraws itself from all objectivity, to become purely interior. This process of interiorization does not stop with the act of faith. Faith too rests on sheer faith, namely, on the belief that I believe. Never will faith possess the certitude of knowledge. The believer can say only: I believe that I have faith. This faith has no support within man himself; its roots are embedded in a world that transcends him. Therefore, it is not an acquired possession, but a continuous striving in fear and trembling. In this sense faith is only *concern* about faith (IX A 32) (763), for this very concern, as extreme objective uncertainty, is the sign of complete interiority. Every certainty seduces the believer from his interior existence into objective "knowledge."

A further consequence of the subjectivity of our relation to God is that the truth of the act of faith is rather in the bearing of the act on its object than in the object itself. *How* we believe is more important than *what* we believe. To know God truly is not to know the true God, but to achieve a true relation to God (PS VII 184-85 LO 178). A Christian who does not pray truly to God is in reality praying to an idol, whereas the heathen who kneels before a false god in spirit and in truth, is adoring the true God (PS VII 186-87 LO 180).

While objective thought is indifferent to the thinking subject and his existence, the subjective thinker is as an existing individual essentially interested in his own thinking, existing as he is in thought (PS VII 60-61 LO 67).

The truth of faith consists in this: that one commit oneself and risk his life for a truth which one does not possess, but which is posited by the commitment itself. This observation leads us to the second characteristic: namely, that the subjectivity of faith can be realized only in a *dialectical process* of ever-increasing interiority. The act of faith necessarily objectifies itself by positing its content as truth; but it can only maintain its distinctive character by returning to the subjective. Thus faith constantly tends to become objective knowledge, but at the same time it keeps detaching itself from its acquired positions by an ever-renewed inward movement. Only such a dialectical faith is authentic for Kierkegaard. So-called immediate faith, in which personal inclinations, culture, and education lead man to a spontaneous and irreflective religious belief, depends entirely upon external circumstances and lacks the essential characteristic of faith: personal commitment. Dialectical or reflective faith, on the contrary, is determined by a subjective attitude which constantly abandons all objective footholds. Despite the more difficult task it involves, this attitude can be demanded of everyone. It only requires courage enough to abandon oneself and to place one's life in God's hands.

Consistent with this theory, Kierkegaard comments on examples of immediate faith in the Gospels, such as those of the centurion and of the woman with the hemorrhage:

Essentially this is not faith, but an immediate surrender to Christ (perhaps not even as Son of God), as to a man who is able to help them, and this immediacy possesses extraordinary endurance. But is this faith? In the final analysis it is not clear whether Christ signifies more than a man who is able to help. If this immediacy is faith, then every young girl in love has faith (IX A 11).

What, then, can we think of Christ's praise of these people for their faith? He Who could read the hearts of men saw that faith would follow this first and spontaneous act of devotion.

Yet, the dialectical character of faith also requires the existence of an object. As we will see later, it is precisely the transcendent reality of the object of faith that makes the act purely subjective. Kierkegaard's subjectivity, for that reason, has nothing in common with the romantic concept of religious feeling which lacks any reference to an object. His subjectivity is the subjectivity of the *will*, which essentially depends on an object. However, he wishes to preserve it from self-satisfied complacency in objective acquisitions. As soon as the object is "assimilated" by the believer, the object of faith ceases to be transcendent, and the act is reduced to an act of cognition. All the emphasis, therefore, is placed on the subjective involvement. A religious truth depends entirely on the free decision by which we make it *our own*.[7]

---

[7] Kierkegaard means that faith cannot affirm its object, except by a personal commitment, a choice, a decision. Cf. H. Bouillard, "La Foi d'après Kierkegaard," *Bulletin de littérature ecclesiastique* (1947), p. 23.

Only a corrupt Christianity can look on the truth of faith as if it were an immediate datum, a result handed down from father to son as a completely acquired possession. The truth of faith is never a result; it is the truth of a *way*. There is only one method for finding it: to follow the way from beginning to end, just as our predecessors did (TC XII 229-30 LO 202).

Consequently, the role of the will is predominant in the act of faith. As early as 1834, Kierkegaard noted:

Faith, surely, implies an act of the will, and moreover not in the same sense as when I say, for instance, that all apprehension implies an act of the will; how can I otherwise explain the saying in the New Testament that whatsoever is not of faith is sin (I A 36) (10).

Insofar as it is an act of the will, faith is opposed to doubt, which is also essentially volitional. Just as the skeptic holds his mind in *suspenso* because he wills it so, so also the man of faith banishes doubt by free decision.

The conclusion of belief is not so much a conclusion as a resolution, and it is for this reason that belief excludes doubt (PF IV 275 LO 69).

From another point of view doubt precedes the act of faith as its necessary condition. Truly to *make a choice* one must first be liberated from every objective necessity; otherwise, faith would not be a free decision (III A 4). Moreover, the doubt preceding faith is not only intellectual but also, to a much greater extent, volitional; it is a doubt about the possibility of returning to God (III A 36).

All the believer has to do is to be concerned solely with himself. But this assignment is quite sufficient for him, for "to become subjective is the most difficult of all tasks" (PS VII 115 LO 116). Man always wants to make history, to play a leading role on the stage of life. But to believe is to choose oneself as the absolute—that is, to choose oneself in the sight of God (SD XI 182 LO 77).

Because of the subjective and volitional character of faith, any direct communication in objective terms becomes impossible. Kierkegaard was fully aware of this; the two principal works in which he treated faith objectively and with intellectual categories appeared under the pseudonym, "Johannes Climacus." Climacus is not a Christian, but one who is *reflecting* on Christianity. His objective approach, although necessary for an intellectual discussion, cannot avoid distorting a reality which is per se subjective. Kierkegaard, therefore, does not want this exposition to be considered as an adequate account of his own innermost experience.

Faith begins with an agonizing leap, not with an intellectual-dialectical transition (VI A 33; cf. also X¹ A 219 (900) and IV C 87-96). As an ethical task it is equally difficult for the learned and for the simple; nay, in this age of reflection which seeks to understand everything, it is more exacting for a scholar than for any other man.

For the simple heart it is simply: thou shalt believe. For the understanding intellect it is: it is against reason, but *thou shalt* believe. Here the *thou shalt* is much stronger, just because it is opposed to something (X A 187; cf. also X A 624).

The struggle of faith against the world is not an ideological but a "character-struggle," in which the issue is not understanding but childlike obedience. Hence, Kierkegaard defines faith as self-defense, by unconditional obedience, against the idle wish to understand and the idle presumption that one can understand (X¹ A 368). Faith is anything but genius—it is sheer work. Or, more correctly, it is love, for only love can believe without objective evidence. The leap

of faith is the risk of love, and the certainty of faith is the
trust in the Beloved. This is the meaning of Christ's word: "I
will make myself known to him who loves me."

At this point the reader may wonder whether Kierkegaard
has not submerged himself in subjectivism. Certain passages
strongly suggest this conclusion. It should be worthwhile,
then, to see how he defends himself against this criticism.

In the first place, faith, of course, is not a matter of those
unaccountable and bizarre forms of subjectivity which everyone, unfortunately, possesses in abundance, but, as we said
before, it is the subjectivity of the will (PS VII 115 LO 117).
Next, Kierkegaard emphasizes that *subjectivity* is by no means
identical with *immanence;* the subject cannot educe the object of faith from within himself as in pantheistic idealism.
On the contrary, Kierkegaard maintains, the highest subjectivity and the most profound interiority become possible
only by reference to a wholly transcendent object. That this
object of faith is not attainable through objective knowledge
is not due to its deficiency but to its transcendence. Thought
remains in the realm of the immanent, but faith leads to the
transcendent. The subjectivity of the act of faith does not
imply that no objective reality corresponds to it, but rather
that the *act itself* proceeds entirely within the realm of
subjectivity.[8] As has been observed, this truth is the same
which Augustine, Pascal, Blondel, and many others are expressing when they call faith a choice depending on the
disposition of the heart.[9]

The whole question now is how the act of faith is connected with its object. We could hardly agree with commentators who see a "danger" in Kierkegaard's work of too
greatly emphasizing the objective aspect of faith,[10] or a

[8] Hirsch, *Kierkegaard-Studien,* p. 754.
[9] Bouillard, *art. cit.,* p. 23.
[10] Ruttenbeck, *Søren Kierkegaard, Der Christliche Denker und sein
Werk,* p. 233.

tendency to replace the Protestant *fides qua* (the interiority of faith) with the Catholic *fides quae* (the content of faith).[11] To us the opposite seems to be true, for Kierkegaard explicitly notes in his diary that there is a how (*qua*) which, once stated with precision, also answers the what (*quae*). This is the *qua* of faith (X² A 299) (1021). Yet it remains true that the subjectivity of the act of faith ultimately results from the transcendence of its *object*. In other words, subjectivity is the only way to approach a divine object. Only by the abandonment of all objectivity does our relationship with God become truly objective. If God is the *Wholly Other,* the only correct attitude toward Him consists in renouncing all objective content to the point where the relation has no content other than itself; complete subjectivity is the only objectively correct approach of God.

Kierkegaard goes further. Not only in its term, but also in its origin, the act of faith is connected with a transcendent object. The pure subjectivity of the act of faith is possible only because the content of the revelation, from which faith begins, "expresses not merely something which man has not given himself, but something that would never have come to the mind of man, not even as a wish, an ideal, or whatever you call it" (II A 517).

Far from reducing the whole content of faith to the living experience of it, Kierkegaard claims that the pure subjectivity of the act is due entirely to the transcendence of its content. Characteristic of faith is not that it has no objectivity, but that the *act itself* (the appropriation) is disengaged from the objec-

---

[11] H. Roos, *Kierkegaard et le Catholicisme* (Louvain, 1955), p. 48. Both judgments seem to be based mainly on a journal entry of 1853 in which Kierkegaard lauds Tertullian for having seen "that faith—*fides objectiva* or *quae creditur*—remains unconditionally the same" (X⁵ A 98). But in this text he wishes only to show that faith does not develop through time; to this point he cites Tertullian, who, at least so far as *fides quae* is concerned, accepted this position.

tive content. Taken by itself, the *subjective* process has no objective content, but this in no way diminishes the objectivity belonging to the content of faith inasmuch as it *precedes appropriation;* it only denies that in the act of faith the content intrinsically determines the *appropriation* of it.

The transcendence of the content of faith implies that it can be communicated only by a revelation. An immanent truth originating from an autonomous subject has no meaning in Christianity, for its truth entirely transcends the subject (IX A 221) (809).

Thus we see that the act of faith does not occur in a vacuum, but is securely attached at either end to a pole of objectivity. However, this only raises a further problem. How can Kierkegaard define the act of faith as pure subjectivity, considering that this act is specified by an object (the content of revelation) which is entirely *given?* In other words, how can the act of faith maintain sufficient freedom in respect to its object so that Kierkegaard can call it pure subjectivity? The answer, once more, must be sought in the very nature of the object of faith. The object of faith is not given *immediately* such that it determines assent.[12] Now the object can fail to determine assent only if the object of faith contains itself something repellent, something paradoxical for the understanding.

When subjectivity, inwardness, is the truth, the truth becomes objectively a paradox; and the fact that the truth is objectively a paradox shows in its turn that subjectivity is the truth (PS VII 190 LO 183).

One wonders how we can believe in what is paradoxical or even absurd. Kierkegaard's answer is simple: How can one

[12] Kierkegaard claims that faith, like philosophy, starts with wonder, but the difference is that in faith wonder keeps increasing instead of diminishing (V A 25).

believe anything except the paradoxical? If the object is not paradoxical, we have left the realm of faith for that of knowledge.

The whole problem, then, amounts to this: Why is the object of religion such that it cannot be known, but must be believed: in other words, why must it be paradoxical? The solution can only be that between a divine revelation and human knowledge there is an unbridgeable gap. A proof for the truth of faith, or even for the existence of God, according to Kierkegaard, ought a priori to be rejected. Immanent thought might perhaps reach God's being (*at vaere*), which in this case, would still be an abstract idea, but never His presence (*at vaere til*). Only for faith is God *existing*, is He really present (VII A 139) (605). This existence never can be the object of rational demonstration; it rests on conviction (*overbevisning*), a notion that goes *beyond* human *proof* (*bevisning*) (VII A 215). In every respect God is the unknown, the limit of our thinking. He is so far removed from us that even His otherness is a matter which we can learn only from God Himself. Nothing divine falls within the scope of human thought (PF IV 237-39 LO 34-36).[13] What causes this absolute difference is a point to which we shall return later. For now, it suffices to say that we are confronted here with an extreme Reformation position: because of sin, any accommodation between God and man has become impossible.

It is precisely this paradoxical character of its object which makes the act of faith purely subjective. Subjectivity increases as the immediate "givenness" of its object decreases; the less the object is given, the more the subject becomes free. Subjectivity reaches its height when the object, in which it has infinite interest, becomes pure uncertainty; at that moment, the subject is moved to genuine passion. That is why

---

[13] All this has not prevented Kierkegaard from providing himself with a proof of the existence of God in *Sickness Unto Death*.

Kierkegaard calls paradox "the passion of thought" (IV A 191).[14] The objective repulsion of the paradox throws the subject back upon itself and forces it to approach its object from within itself with no other foothold than its own *interestedness*—passion. In the presence of paradox, truth (whatever meaning this word retains in a process which is liberation from all objectivity) is entirely displaced toward the interior, the subject. Kierkegaard then defines faith as "objective uncertainty, due to the repulsion of the absurd[15] held fast by the passion of inwardness" (PS VII 602 LO 540).

3. *Christ, the Absolute Paradox of Faith*

Thus far we have made no distinction between simple paradox and what Kierkegaard calls "the absolute paradox," or "the absurd." We have learned that there are two types of religion: Socratic and Christian. Socrates was the first to realize that every knower is primarily an *existing subject*— that is, a free being placed in a certain time and situation. Consequently, truth is primarily a personal affair; it originates within the existential interiority of the knower. Given this starting point, all truth, as the objective correlate of this interiorization is, to a certain extent, paradoxical, for the objective always presents itself as a challenge to a subject which is pure interiority. The more vital its importance to the subject, the more stubbornly objective truth resists interiorization. For this reason, God, who is Absolute Truth, is a complete paradox for Socrates.

[14] No more than "thought" here is to be understood in a strictly intellectual sense, does "passion" signify sensuous passion; it refers to spiritual passion, that is, the motion of the spirit no longer supported by the object in which it has an extreme interest.
[15] The absurd means absolute paradox, as will be explained in the next section.

Indeed, when existence (that is, being in and through time) stands in a relationship of truth to Eternity, then the task of integration can never be completed. Yet in the attempt the subject realizes its own highest truth, subjectivity. Thus for him whose norm of truth is the subjective, faith is the ground for every deeper understanding. However, since the paradoxical element in Socratic truth is due solely to the subject, not to the object in itself as it is in Christian faith, Kierkegaard continues calling Socratic faith "knowledge."

The eternal essential truth is [for Socrates] by no means in itself a paradox; but it becomes paradoxical by virtue of its relationship to an existing individual. The Socratic ignorance gives expression to the objective uncertainty attaching to the truth, while his inwardness in existing is the truth (PS VII 190 LO 183).

For Socrates, paradox is only objective ignorance. But a new element enters into the Christian perspective. If the relationship of the eternal truth to an existing subject was already paradoxical in a Socratic perspective, it becomes an absolute paradox in the Christian situation where Eternity and the existing subject are totally disproportionate (PS VII 195 LO 188). What is responsible for this absolute diversity between God and man? After all, man is a creature of God; he should have some likeness to Him. The answer is that man himself has deliberately cut off his relation with God in an act of supreme independence—sin (PF IV 240 LO 37). In sin man has withdrawn himself from God so utterly that he cannot even perceive the separation between God and himself, for a separation still presupposes a relation.

It follows that any contact between God and man is not only paradoxical, but absolutely paradoxical—or absurd.

When Socrates believed that there was a God, he held fast to the objective uncertainty with the passion of his inwardness and it is precisely in this contradiction and in this risk that faith is rooted. Now it is otherwise. Instead of the objective uncertainty, there is here a certainty, namely, that objectively it is absurd; and this absurdity held fast in the passion of inwardness, is faith (PS VII 195-96 LO 188).

The absurdity of faith is that God, despite the total otherness of man (which results from sin), nevertheless enters into a relation with him. Revelation and redemption, by which God comes into contact with man, become contradictions in the situation of sin.

With this absolute paradox, faith has reached the summit of interiority. For Socrates also, subjectivity had been truth, but his very confidence of achieving truth by subjectivity had placed him in constant danger of falling back on objectivism. This danger is avoided by the Christian concept of sin; in it, subjectivity becomes *untruth*. Guilty before God, man becomes untrue to the depths of his being; thus, the last refuge for the objective, which was located in subjectivity itself, is closed off (PS VII 195 LO 188).

The absolute paradox has still another side. To reveal man's sinful state and subsequent redemption, God made Himself like man: the Eternal became incarnate in time.

Thus our paradox is rendered still more appalling, or the same paradox has the double aspect which proclaims it as the absolute paradox; negatively by revealing the absolute unlikeness of sin, positively by proposing to do away with the absolute unlikeness in absolute likeness (PF IV 241 LO 37).

Man's relationship with God, despite His otherness, retained a certain negative immanence. Now it becomes entirely transcendent: as another man He takes his place in history beside me, and becomes external to me. This is the depth of the mystery of Christ, that God as a particular indi-

vidual in time transforms man in his subjectivity. Every effort
to understand God in His Incarnation is vain. Speculative
understanding is powerless before this absolute paradox. To
explain it is to destroy it: the only valid explanation is that
it is inexplicable (PS VII 205 LO 197).

The eternal happiness of the individual is decided in time
through the relationship to something historical, which is furthermore of such a character as to include in its composition that
which by virtue of its essence cannot become historical, and must
therefore become such by virtue of an absurdity (PS VII 374 LO
345).

The paradox of the Incarnation consists not in some
vaguely metaphysical unity between God and man as such,
but in a personal identity of God and this particular man—
Christ. Christ's humanity is a concrete reality of flesh and
blood. Kierkegaard is very much opposed to any sort of
Docetism (sham Incarnation). For him Christ is the subsistent
ambiguity of a man who is God.

That is why He is necessarily paradoxical and could communicate Himself only as object of faith (TC XII 43 LO 29).

The coming of Christ is and remains a paradox. To his contemporaries the paradox lay in the fact that he, this particular
individual man who looked like other men, spoke like them,
followed their habits and customs, was the son of God. To later
generations the paradox is different; for as they do not see him
with their physical eye it is easier to imagine him as the son of
God, and then that which gives offence and scandal is that he
adopted the habit of mind of a particular age (IV A 47) (417).

Christ's divinity is impervious to sense and understanding.
Observers were unable to detect it even in His most obviously miraculous deeds (X³ A 19).

What the Jews, and later many others, asked of Christ: that he should prove his divinity, is preposterous; for, if he really were the Son of God the proof would be ridiculous, just as ridiculous as though a man were to prove his existence, since in this case, Christ's existence and his divinity are the same (I A 53) (14).

Christ is not a king who disguised himself as a servant, only to reveal his identity at the right moment (PF IV 247-48 LO 44-45). His Incarnation is irrevocable; becoming man, God as it were forever renounced the possibility of abandoning His incognito.

The paradox of the person of Christ, as Kierkegaard understands it, emphasizes the strictly personal character of the act of faith. Christianity is not a doctrine, but a Person to Whom I entrust myself without reserve. In Christianity the Master cannot render Himself superfluous, as he can in Socratic education. Faith is so related to the Master that it stands or falls with Him (PF IV 254 LO 50). A doctrine once taught is appropriated independently of the instructor. To understand a doctrine is to appropriate it. But the principles of Christianity can never be understood independently of the Person of Christ. To understand Christ's words "by themselves"—that is, as a doctrine—is to discount the element from which they receive their basic meaning, the divinity of their speaker. For the true believer it is a blasphemy to say that Christ's words are wise or profound, for that puts them on a par with human philosophies and takes away the transcendence of Him who proclaimed them.

For this reason Kierkegaard rejects Luther's position which disregards the person of the teacher in evaluating the doctrine he presents.

Luther should be a little more cautious. The fact is that Christianity entered the world in a quite different way, so that the person is above the doctrine. How can one come to know whether such-and-such a point is the word or doctrine of God? If Luther answers, "By examining the doctrine . . . ," then all is lost and Christianity becomes nothing more than a human invention. Quite the opposite occurs when I bow to another's authority. But then the person becomes more important than the doctrine (X^2 A 448).

Here one might object that in any direct communication the words, if they are to have meaning at all, can be understood by themselves. In a direct communication, yes, but Christ cannot directly communicate His doctrine to us (TC XII 145 LO 123). For all direct communication the one who communicates must be known. But in taking human nature, God has chosen an incognito that cannot be set aside. What Christ seems to be differs from what He is. Even His most direct utterances become indirect; His divine nature, from which His communication receives its real meaning, necessarily remains hidden—He cannot take off His incognito (X^2 A 367).[16] Here is a Man reviled and cursed by all, condemned as a criminal, and nailed to a cross; when this Man says, "Believe in Me, I am God," then His claim, however direct, is most indirect (X^3 A 181). Therefore, every word He speaks and every act He performs receives its meaning only from the stand we take toward His person. It cannot be immediately understood and appropriated, but poses a task to the hearer or the observer, the task to define one's attitude toward Christ. To be understood Christ's words have to be *believed,* that is, to be connected with the living Paradox who proclaimed them, and who Himself cannot be understood, but only believed in.

[16] According to Kierkegaard, only in the Resurrection and in the Ascension is there direct communication, for only in these cases does Divinity reveal itself. It would seem to me, however, that Christ's communication is as direct in His miracles as in those two mysteries: the hidden is revealed.

One can fully believe only in a person in the present, in a contemporary. Christ, however, lived and died many hundreds of years ago. To establish a genuine relation of belief, therefore, we must somehow bridge the ages which separate us from Him. There cannot be any distance between Him and us, particularly since the very conditions of our faith in Christ cannot be received at second hand. Christ Himself has to create within each of His disciples the conditions necessary for "understanding" Him (PF IV 294 LO 85-86). History, therefore, can have no place in the act of faith. Of course, a few historical data are necessary to make a genuine faith in Christ possible. Once there lived a man who claimed to be God and worked miraculous signs. For this point, but only for this, we admit the mediating function of contemporary reports. But what we thus receive is only the *occasion* and not the cause for arousing a personal act of faith. The role of contemporary witnesses is very limited. Even their general veracity is irrelevant; it is enough for us to learn this one fact—that the Godhead dwelt on earth in human form (PF IV 295 LO 87).

History can be no help in matters of faith. Apologists have time and again tried to demonstrate Christ's divinity from history. The success crowning His work, the triumph achieved by His Church, and like arguments have been developed to offset the profound humiliations suffered by God Incarnate. But the mystery of the Cross can never be removed by subsequent historical facts. History, therefore, should not try to make amends to Christ. He Himself willed these humiliations; it is blasphemy to think they were due to unfortunate circumstances of the moment and have been compensated for by later ages (TC XII 51 LO 37).

To approach Christ, a trans-historical relationship is required. The Jew of the year A. D. 30 was not closer to Him than we: we both face the same paradox, and undoubtedly

Jesus' contemporaries were more tempted by the deceptive testimony of the senses than those who never knew Him as a carpenter's son (PF IV 279-80 LO 72-73).

Only faith makes one a true contemporary of Christ, for faith alone leads to the *praesentia Christi*. As long as there is one believer in the world, Christ remains contemporaneous (TC XII 19 LO 9). And, conversely, nothing but the contemporary presence of Christ makes true faith possible; for, to surrender to Christ, we must first face Him and ask ourselves: "How would I have acted if I had lived in His day?" Only to the contemporary of Christ does the paradox appear.

No more than the history of Christianity can the miracles of Christ ever mitigate the paradox of His person. Surely Christ did not intend "to pass through the world in such a manner that no single human being becomes aware of his presence" (PF IV 248 LO 44). His miracles drew attention to Him. But are they proof for His divinity? Certainly not as a geometric theorem is proven, for then we would all be convinced without faith.

Let us see what Christ Himself had to say about this. The Gospel reports how the emissaries of John the Baptist came to ask Jesus whether He was the one who was to come. His answer was: "The blind see, the lame walk, the lepers are cleansed, the deaf hear, the poor have the Gospel preached to them. And blessed is he who is not scandalized in Me" (Mt 2, 1-6). Kierkegaard interprets this passage in the following manner:

Christ's reply comprises in *contento* all that commonly goes by the name of "proofs" for the truth of Christianity . . . He points to the miracles (the lame walk, the blind see, etc.) and to the doctrine itself (the Gospel is preached to the poor)—and thereupon, strangely enough, He adds, "Blessed is he whosoever is not offended in Me"—But behold how different is the custom in

Christendom! There they have written these huge folios which develop the proofs of the truth of Christianity. Behind these proofs and folios they feel perfectly confident and secure from every attack; for the proofs and the folios regularly conclude with the assurance, Ergo Christ was what He said He was; by the aid of the proofs this conclusion is just as sure as that 2 and 2 make 4, and just as easy as thrusting the foot into the stocking; supported by this incontrovertible ergo, which makes the matter directly evident, the docents and the parsons strut, and the missionaries go forth to convert the heathen with the help of this ergo. How different was it with Christ! He does not say, *Ergo* I am the expected one—He says (after having appealed to the proofs) "blessed is he whosoever is not offended in Me" (TC XII 116-17 LO 97-98).

All these proofs, then, make it no less necessary to take a personal stand with respect to Christ. After seeing a miracle, the mind still wavers and one must choose. Only the choice itself will determine one's faith in Christ. Miracles are never immediate proofs of Christ's divinity. The very fact that we need them implies that we are unable to recognize Christ immediately, and only if we could recognize God immediately in Christ would there be an immediate proof of His divinity (TC XII 117 LO 98). What then is the role of miracles? They focus attention on Christ. The signs that Christ performed bring man to a point where he can no longer overlook the paradox of His person and where he has to take a stand for or against Him. But at the same time they create the possibility of being scandalized.

Thought and the absolute paradox of faith cannot meet without arousing the *possibility* of scandal. The absence of this possibility would only indicate that we have not yet reached the paradox, the point where genuine faith begins. Modern theology has tried to suppress scandal by arguing the harmony between thought and the object of faith. But this is a blunder, for by removing the paradox from faith it has made faith itself impossible. The only result of such efforts is that Christianity is left without Christians.

Since faith is a complete self-surrender, it scandalizes not only the intellect but the entire moral person. Before achieving the fullness of faith man must first have faced despair. As Kierkegaard shows in *Sickness unto Death,* the absolute choice of faith always appears as an alternative to despair. That is why sin, which in its extreme form is always a choice of despair, is opposed, not to virtue, but to faith.

Only against a background of despair and doubt, the basic objects of faith, Providence and redemption take on their full significance. Faith is in the same dialectical tension with despair as it is with doubt: they eliminate each other, because they represent opposite attitudes of the will, but by the same token they are also found to be singularly close to one another, as two alternatives of one existential dilemma.[17]

4. *Faith and Reason*

After all that has preceded, the reader may well wonder whether there is any room left for reason in Kierkegaard's theory of faith. Could there be any apologetics of a faith which is based entirely on paradox?

To answer this question it might be good to point out first that Kierkegaard's purpose was basically apologetic. He reexamined the stages of consciousness to bring to light the possibility of an authentic act of faith. His entire work should be regarded as an effort, by means of a more profound meditation on the experience of modern man, to rediscover the commensurability of faith with reflective thought (X^2 A 622).[18]

[17] Cf. H. Diem, *Philosophie und Christentum bei S. Kierkegaard* (Munich, 1929), p. 296.
[18] Anz, *op. cit.,* p. 10.

This commensurability, Kierkegaard finds, is based not on a rationalistic coincidence of faith with reason, but on the limitation of reason itself. The error of idealism is not that it carries reflection too far, but on the contrary that it fails to carry it far enough (X^1 A 330).

Idealism halts where the existential synthesis of the finite and the infinite occurs; thus it fails to explain the ultimate ground of this synthesis: the infinite. Kierkegaard carries through his own reflection, down to the very ground for the experience of the infinite: absolute subjectivity.[19] In contrast with idealism, the dialectic of subjectivity demonstrates that the more profound reflection leads man not to identity, but to opposition with the Divine. It concludes in man's awareness of himself as guilty before God.

Consequently basing his procedure on reflection itself, Kierkegaard has opened the way to a transcendent terminus. Man is no longer the closed, self-sufficient spirit which develops itself through history as a finite-infinite absolute. The finite and the infinite components of the spirit are in disproportion with each other, because man has cut himself off from the Infinite, the very source of his existence as a spirit. Kierkegaard has not justified faith by human thought; rather, he has shown, by means of a deeper reflection on existence itself, that thought necessarily falls short of responding to the question about the ultimate ground of existence. Reflection on the essence of the self, the subjectivity, shows that only an act which goes beyond objective thought can reveal man's innermost nature: his relation to the source of his existence. Such an act is faith: it originates from the depths of the self which lie beyond any objectivation.

Thus faith, instead of being pre-reflective, is seen to be beyond reason, and accessible only by a reflection that penetrates more deeply into human reality than objective thought

[19] *Ibid.*, p. 28.

ever does. This analysis of faith forces reason to acknowledge that faith, far from being superficial and nonreflective, proceeds from a more profound reflection on reality than reason. Thus, as a person who has locked his door and thrown away the key, Kierkegaard has lodged the Christian categories in a reflection so deep that no intellectual argument can ever again take hold of them. Henceforth, faith is only a matter of choice: Do you wish to believe, or not? (X^3 A 209).

People have always thought that reflection would destroy Christianity, and is its natural enemy. I hope I have shown, with God's aid, that religious reflection can retie the knot which a superficial reflection has unraveled for so many years. The authority of the Bible, and all that belongs to it, have been abolished, and it looks as if one were only waiting for the ultimate stage of reflection to clear up everything. But see how, on the contrary, reflection is going to render service by putting springs under Christianity again, and in such a way that it is able to hold out against reflection. Christianity of course remains completely unchanged; not a jot has been altered. But the struggle has become different: previously it was only between reflection and immediate simple Christianity; now it is between reflection and simplicity armed by reflection. . . . The real task is not to understand Christianity but *to understand that one cannot understand it.* That is the sacred cause of faith, and reflection is sanctified by being used for it (IX A 248).

One cannot call this argumentation "apologetic," in the strict sense of the word; Kierkegaard himself calls it "the opposite of apologetic" (IX A 253), because it demonstrates the impossibility of rational justification for religious truth. Nevertheless, such "anti-apologetic" thinking has an apologetic purpose, inasmuch as it justifies faith for reflection. To his first important confrontation with rationalist theology, the *Philosophical Fragments,* Kierkegaard at one time considered adding the subtitle, "Apologetic Prolegomena of Dogmatics, or Approaches of Thought to Faith." In this sense he is to be ranked with the author of *"Credo quia absurdum,"* who became one of Christianity's first apologists.

Finally, it is important to note that Kierkegaard purposely emphasized the *via negationis* in reaction against the rationalistic theology of the nineteenth century. In doing so, he merely followed the method used by Tertullian and Nicholas of Cusa. This process of negation by no means obviates the positive process. In the *Philosophical Fragments,* which is Kierkegaard's most paradoxical work, he sets out to prove that in the case of divine revelation man's attention must be fastened upon it in a very special way. This is the role of the sign. Without being a substitute for faith, for it is not a proof, the sign at least leads man to the point at which he must either believe or turn away from faith. Kierkegaard says explicitly:

God did not assume the form of a servant to make a mockery of men; hence it cannot be his intention to pass through the world in such manner that no single human being becomes aware of his presence. He will therefore doubtless give some sort of sign, though every understanding resting upon an accommodation is essentially without value for one who does not receive the condition (PF IV 248 LO 44).

The function of apologetics is not to prove the truths of faith, but only to make them an inescapable issue. This role is extremely modest and Kierkegaard is the more anxious to keep it within its proper proportions, since the theology of his time was imbued with rationalism. But he does not eliminate all positive indications that lead toward faith, as appears clearly enough from the text cited above, and from several diary entries in the style of the following:

This is how I—and all the world besides—set to work. It is possible that I might begin with a motive, but that is only an inferior stage. Then it is necessary to make one's choice; under the weight of our responsibility before God, there arises a conviction that comes from God (X[1] A 481).

More important than its function in the preparation of faith is the role of reason in the reflection upon faith.[20] Since faith is paradoxical, reason is assigned the negative but indispensable task of pointing up the incomprehensibility of faith. Consequently, reason must know precisely what is and what is not outside its competence, and such knowledge is a prerequisite for defining with accuracy the sphere of faith. Instead of dispelling the mysteriousness of faith, reason must set itself the task of bringing it into relief. This requires that it be able to distinguish between the contradictory and the incomprehensible.

Nonsense therefore he [the believer] cannot believe against the understanding. For precisely the understanding will discern that it is nonsense and will prevent him from believing it; but he makes so much use of the understanding that he becomes aware of the incomprehensible, and then he holds to this, believing against the understanding (PS VII 559 LO 504).

However, Kierkegaard fails to explain *how* reason should make this distinction, and the strongly anti-intellectualistic terms in which he defined the paradox of faith make me doubt whether he would still be able to justify the task which he assigns to reason.

[20] Cf. C. Fabro, "Foi et raison dans l'oeuvre de Kierkegaard," *Revue des Sciences philosophiques et théologiques,* 32 (1948), p. 169-206.

V

THE IMITATION OF CHRIST

1. Christ, the Fulfillment of the Law

GOD IS LOVE and this love pursues man to the point at which it overtakes him: in the depths of sin. Thus the course of man's sin determines the history of God's love. God came seeking man in man's own sinful nature: He Himself became man.

In order that the union [between God and man] may be brought about, God must therefore become the equal of man, and so He will appear in the likeness of the humblest. But the humblest is one who must serve others, and God will therefore appear in the form of a *servant*. But this servant-form is no mere outer garment, like the beggar-cloak of the king (dressed up in order to love a beggar-girl) which therefore flutters loosely about him and betrays the king. . . . It is his true form and figure. For this is the unfathomable nature of love that it desires equality with the beloved, not in jest merely but in earnest and truth. . . . The servant-form was no mere outer garment, and therefore God must suffer all things, endure all things, make experience of all things. He must suffer hunger in the desert, He must thirst in the time of His agony, He must be forsaken in death, absolutely like the humblest—behold the man! His suffering is not that of His death, but His entire life is a story of suffering; and it is love that suffers, the love that gives all is itself in want. . . . The servant-form was no mere outer garment; hence God must yield his spirit in death and again leave the earth (PF IV 225-26 LO 24-26).[1]

This text expresses, better than any commentary, the meaning for Kierkegaard of the Incarnation, the supreme revelation of God's love. In Christ, God has united Himself to us so inseparably that it is no longer possible to distinguish His nature adequately from our own.[2] Kierkegaard never questioned Christ's divinity. For him even the idea of a kenosis, in which Christ through an act of total annihilation empties Himself of His divinity, is unthinkable.

At all times, Christ is as much God as man—just as in the sea the reflection of the sky retains the depth of the celestial vault (II A 595).

The Incarnation is an event in heaven as well as on earth (II A 594). In Christ, God meets man *personally.* Henceforth every man, whenever and wherever he lives, has a personal relationship with God. The reality of the Incarnation, which we usually fail to appreciate because we do not realize that God came into the world *for each one of us,* so greatly surpasses all human categories that the mere thought of it would be the most heinous crime of human pride, had not God

[1] Kierkegaard also refers repeatedly in his diary to Christ's very genuinely human character—e.g., the note of anxiety in what He says to Judas: "What thou dost, do quickly" (II A 258) (221).

[2] Kierkegaard rejects a priori any attempt to understand the union between God and man in Christ, because it is a union between God and just this particular man. Such a relationship is pure paradox, and any speculation about it is impossible (PF IV *passim;* cf. also Thust, *Kierkegaard Der Dichter des Religiösen,* pp. 348-49, 381).

Himself revealed it to us. But God brought about the Incarnation not to show the greatness of man, but the greatness
of His own love (VIII A 648) (752). That is why an explanation of the Incarnation like Hegel's, which attempts to make
God's free act of love a necessary moment in the development
of the Spirit, and thus eliminates the qualitative distinction
between God and man, is for Kierkegaard the "most dreadful
of all blasphemies" (SD XI 256-57 LO 192-93).

Such a conception of the Incarnation directly contradicts
the reality of man's sinfulness. In the second chapter we
saw that sin is a free act by which man takes a stand against
God and decisively breaks off contact with Him. No amount
of progress on man's part will ever enable him to bridge the
chasm which he himself has created. If a new relationship is
ever going to be forged, it cannot originate from a mediation
of the spirit with itself, but only from a supreme act of God's
omnipotence uniting two realities that have become contradictory. The Incarnation is brought about not by internal
compulsion, but by a self-contained and free act of God's
love (PF IV 218 LO 18). God alone determines the instant
in which Eternity becomes time. For man the Incarnation
is a mere fact; he has contributed nothing to it, and it has
entered history not as a result of, but *in spite of* man's historical evolution.

Because of the qualitative distinction between God and
man, God's love will at first make man unhappy.

Humanly speaking, we must be unhappy, because of the disproportion between man and God; and yet what bliss! (IX A 88).

It is very painful for a creature to be beloved of God. For
love strives to attain perfect identity, and this is dreadful
indeed for sinful man. God's love portends for man the down-
fall of his sinful existence. He instinctively dreads any in-

timate association with God, for he knows that God's love is a terrible thing (VIII A 63) (649).

Christ's Incarnation became as much a judgment on this world as a redemption.[3] Christ could bestow His love only in a spirit of truth, and this truth was man's sinfulness. Therefore, He who was love itself had to allow mankind to commit the greatest crime of all time against His own person. In the taking of Jesus' life is revealed the decisive truth about man: his fundamental corruption (VIII A 469). Only through the death of His Son could God resume contact with man. The night on which Jesus was betrayed, we learned that we are all sinners. Not only Judas, but all of us, betrayed the Lord.

Since Christ was the God-man, the meaning of His crucifixion cannot be that the Jews happened, by chance, to be perverse at that time, and Christ, so to speak, an unfortunate victim of circumstance. No, what happened to Christ is of universal character, it demonstrates the obduracy of the whole human race; the same thing will always happen to Him. Christ can never express anything fortuitous (VIII A 145).

Not the guilt of the Jews, but of mankind, of each one of us, was revealed in Christ's death. True, we might not have crucified Him, but we would have denied Him as did Peter, or we would have fled as the other Apostles did. And cowardly unfaithfulness in friends is worse than blind hatred in enemies (CD X 328-33 LO 283-88).

Only Christ had the right to manifest the truth of human corruption by permitting such a crime. No man is allowed to provoke his fellowmen, by his message, to guilt for his death,

---

[3] Christ's worst suffering consisted in the knowledge that His appearance on earth merely scandalized people and condemned them (see PF IV 225-26 LO 25, and especially TC XII 160 LO 138). Kierkegaard calls this the "infinite sadness" of Christ's life (X[3] A 366).

since no man can ever speak the ultimate truth about man
(RDT XI 91-92 LO 113-14). But as God Christ was the
Truth. Therefore He had to express it in an absolute way,
even if countless men were destined thereby to become guilty
(RDT XI 105 LO 130).[4] In His death on the Cross, far more
than in the miracles, Kierkegaard sees the "proof" of Jesus'
divinity (X¹ A 328).

Because His death convicted man of the greatest possible
sin, attack on God, Christ fulfilled the purpose of the Law
to the letter, for "the Law intervened that the offense might
abound" (Rom. 5, 20).

But He has done more than fulfill the law, for when He said:
It is consummated—that was not His last word, but He also
prayed for His enemies, and that belongs to the Gospel (II A 388).

And so Christ reveals Himself as our Redeemer in the very
sentence which He hands down against us (II A 261): the
truth for which He gave His life is still, in the end, the truth
of His love. God's judgment on man and His love for him
coincide in the death of Christ. His death is the ultimate
manifestation of man's sin, but it also marks the beginning of
man's redemption (RDT XI 106 LO 134).

He made requital for what people did against Him! They crucified Him—in requital, His death upon the cross is the sacrifice
of propitiation for the sin of the world, also for this of crucifying

---

[4] In an early draft of *Has a Man the Right to Let Himself Be Put
to Death for the Truth?* Kierkegaard adds that Christ did everything
He could to avoid direct persecution, precisely to diminish the oppor-
tunities for human guilt (VIII A 271). Whether the Christian, coming
after Christ, has the right to suffer death for the absolute truth of
Christianity (not, of course, for any *personal* truth of his) is a question
which occupied Kierkegaard's mind for a long time and which we shall
discuss below.

Him! They betray Him—in requital He institutes the supper of reconciliation for all (CD X 333 LO 288) [slightly corrected].

With divine mercy, Christ took pity on the wickedness which, with divine severity, He revealed. His was the perfect fulfillment of the words of St. Peter's Epistle, "Charity covers a multitude of sins" (1 Pt 4, 8). In one and the same act God condemned man totally and then, by transferring the entire condemnation to Himself, redeemed him completely. Christ has become sin in our place. He has borne the curse of sin that we might be saved, and has endured death that we might live. We stepped aside that He might take our place.

When then revenging justice in its judgment here in this world or in the hereafter seeks out the place where I, a sinner, should stand with all my guilt, with my many sins, then it will not find me; I stand no longer in that place; I have forsaken it; in my place there stands Another, Another who puts Himself at stake for me; saved, I stand beside the Other, beside Him, my Redeemer (HP XI 290; cf. also IX A 269).[5]

In His Son's death we possess a token of God's unchangeable love. The immutability of God's love is the one a priori conviction inaccessible to attack from without, that will support the Christian throughout the trials of life (VIII A 25) (640). In 1851, exhausted and embittered by controversy, Kierkegaard delivered a sermon in the Copenhagen Citadel Church which he was to publish as his final religious message. God's love—runs the theme of the discourse—is not like a spring

---

[5] With Chestov, we detect in the above passage an echo of God's address to His only begotten Son in the writings of Luther: "Be thou Peter the betrayer, Paul the persecutor, the blasphemer, and the man of violence, David the adulterer, the sinner who ate the apple in Paradise, the murderer on the cross, be Thou the Person Who hath committed all the sins in the world." Chestov, *Kierkegaard et la philosophie existentielle,* p. 368.

at which a traveler has once found refreshment and which he now revisits, many years later, only to find it dried up; God's love continues to flow, it does not remain behind even when the traveler passes on, but instead accompanies him— what is more, it goes seeking him when he is lost. And the meditation closes with this prayer:

Whenever any human being comes to Thee, of whatever age, at whatever time of the day, in whatever state: if he comes in sincerity he always finds Thy love equally warm, like the spring's unchanged coolness, O Thou who are unchangeable! Amen! (UG XIV 306 LO 240; cf. also IX A 374).

Living faith in God's love, however, requires that one relive the Gospel as a *contemporary*. The notion of the *contemporary*, which was still abstract in the dialectic of faith, now receives concrete content and meaning: by His grace and reconciliation Christ has really come as close to us as He was to His contemporaries. At this stage faith in Christ becomes prayer, for only in prayer can we express that God has become everything for us and at the same time infinitely transcends us (PS VII 401 LO 369). Not everything requested in prayer is granted: the opposition between God and man is too great for that. Since this opposition stems from man's sinfulness, while his true interests lie on God's side, man can win only by surrendering unconditionally to God. In a struggle with God, only defeat is triumph. Kierkegaard develops this theme masterfully in his *Edifying Discourses* of 1844: "The righteous man strives in prayer with God and conquers—in that God conquers" (ED V 168-92 LO IV 113-43).

The important point is not, as we might suppose, whether the favors requested are granted. True prayer begins when solicitude for such trifles ceases; it consists in the relationship

with God itself.⁶ Does prayer, then, alter anything? Could
man's prayer really cause God *to change?* To this Kierkegaard replies: Yes, God has changed, precisely in *showing* that
He is immutable.

Yet this immutability is not that icy indifference, that destructive
elevation, that ambiguous aloofness, which the hardened understanding eulogized; on the contrary, this immutability is heart-
felt and warm and omnipresent, an immutability that concerns
itself about a man's welfare, and, just on that account, does per-
mit itself to be changed by the cries of a petitioner, as if everything were now over; by his cowardice, when he finds it most
convenient not to be able to help himself; by his false contrite-
ness which he immediately regrets as soon as the momentary
anxiety of the danger is over (ED V 184 LO IV 134).

Man too has changed in the course of his prayer, for if he
has prayed well, his prayer always ends with "amen," that
is, with complete surrender to God's will. Indeed, during his
prayer the important point has become God Himself, and
that for which he was praying has been returned to its proper
place in God's plan of salvation (ED V 184 LO IV 133). The
ideal is to pray, not until God hears what we ask of Him,
but until we hear what God asks of us (VII A 56) (572). It
is wrong to finish a prayer with the expectation that, from
now on, "things will go better." For what is "better"? Is it
what we find more attractive? To thank God for that is a
step backward in the spiritual life, because we thereby bring
Him down to our own level. If it is true that God does well
whatever He does, then such prayer is meaningless (V A 46)

⁶ Kierkegaard here cites Saint Teresa's words, which he found quoted
in Fénelon's writings: "Oh, how blind are those who abandon prayer
just when they ought to begin it!" (X¹ A 291). For that matter, the
miracle of being able to *ask* God should cause one to forget whether
or not the prayer has been *answered* (SL VI 367 LO 320; also IX A
192 [802]).

(489). The true purpose of prayer is to transform not the world but oneself.

The real difficulty with prayer, therefore, is to say "Amen" at the end and to mean what one says. Few achieve the ultimate, total surrender to which authentic prayer should lead. Many say "Amen," but add a secret sigh of wistfulness for themselves. The ideal of prayer is "to say *Amen* so that there is not one word more, not a single one, to add, but that, rather, the only one that contents and satisfies is this Amen!" (IX A 24). That is the summit of prayer of supplication, and Kierkegaard believes that every prayer ultimately should be prayer of supplication, for a sinner can hardly afford not to plead again and again for God's mercy. Prayer is the supreme admission of one's own helplessness.

The Christian craves only to be satisfied with God's grace; he does not ask that he may help himself, but prays for God's grace, nor does he ask that God should help him otherwise than as God wills, he prays only to be satisfied with God's grace. The Christian has no self-will, he surrenders unconditionally. . . . He accepts everything by God's grace . . . even the grace itself; he understands that he cannot do without God's grace even in praying for his grace (CD X 80 LO 67).

In the process of redemption the point is not to *do,* but to *let* it *be done,* and this attitude of total surrender to God is expressed in the active passivity of prayer. We can contribute nothing to what must happen anyway. All we need do is to submit ourselves (IX A 358). However passive it seems, this surrender requires more effort than the most exhausting activity (VIII A 202).

The surrender of faith implies a demand for obedience, far more exacting than the imperatives of an immanent morality.

Whoever does not place himself in a relationship of total surrender, does not relate himself to God at all. In this relationship
one cannot go only to a certain point, for God is just the opposite
of what goes only to a certain point (X^2 A 644).

The surrender of faith is a surrender to the absolute and
therefore involves the whole man.[7] It introduces a new ethics,
the ethics of faith.

2. *The Ethics of Interiority*

How, then, should we envisage the new ethics of Christianity? In the first place, man is again faced with the task
of actualizing the natural law. God's law, written within the
creature, could be suspended, but never abolished. The general law to which man previously had been subject, as to
an immanent obligation, now becomes part of his transcendent relationship with the Absolute (FT III 162 LO 151).
If God wishes to enter into contact with man, this must be
done on the basis of man's own concrete reality, that is,
according to the law of his nature. In the context of man's
new relationship with God, the natural law acquires a religious significance. Exceptions in the name of religion (e.g.
the one that was made for Abraham) are no longer possible,
for the law itself has become religion. But the relationship
with the Absolute in faith has changed the whole perspective
of ethics: from now on, its fundamental principle will be to
give the absolute, absolute consideration, and the relative,
only relative consideration (PS VII 403 LO 369-70).

In practice this means that henceforth the believer will
attempt to serve one Master alone. God is no longer the

[7] Cf. C. Manzia, "Il problema della fede in Kierkegaard," *Problemi
scelti di Teologia contemporanea* (Rome, 1954), pp. 123-32.

principal concern of his life (as in the first type of ethics); He is the only concern. Christian life must be molded according to the rule: No man can serve two masters (Mt 6, 24) (JY XII 487-550 LO 161-217).[8] Christ's example should teach Christians to have wives as if they had none, to weep as though not weeping, to rejoice as though not rejoicing, to buy as though not possessing, and to use this world as though not using it (I Cor 7, 29-31).

This attitude does not reject worldly values, for that would be only a negative way of considering the relative as absolute, whereas the ethical ideal is to regard the absolute absolutely, and the relative relatively. By rejecting earthly things, medieval asceticism attached greater importance to them than they deserved and thus posited them as a negative absolute opposed to God. The infinite distance between absolute and relative ends is not sufficiently recognized in a dualistic opposition which treats them as equal partners. On the contrary, the correct attitude for a Christian is always to see relative ends in the light of the absolute, and to show love for God, as He indicated we should by placing us in this world. One who bypasses earthly things to seek an immediate relationship with God denies the infinite distance between God and man (PS VII 401-02 LO 369). Such a person does not fully accept God's dominion: to the accepting of things as God has disposed them, he prefers the security of not being distracted from the absolute.

Here is a dialectical problem. It may be a tribulation, but it may also be true: that a man demands too much of God, desires to be altogether too spiritual, and so in a sense wants to love God more or otherwise than God allows, if in relation to all his suffering

---

[8] Geismar correctly summarizes the idea of this discourse about *Christ as Example,* when he says that the only important human element in the remission of sins is the honesty to will only one thing, in *S. Kierkegaard* (p. 516).

and temptation he only ever wishes to be helped spiritually. There are certain innocent human expedients (distractions, physical recreation) which a man may not overlook without asking too much of God (X¹ A 452) (924).

Thus the new ethics becomes primarily an internal attitude. An outsider cannot tell whether someone agrees to the things of this world in an absolute, or in a relative way. What is specifically Christian is for the most part hidden, and "those who carry the jewel of faith are likely to be delusive, because their outward appearance bears a stunning resemblance to that which both the infinite resignation and faith profoundly despise . . . philistinism" (FT III 100 LO 52). Like anybody else in Copenhagen, the Christian will go to Dyrehaven[9] on a Sunday afternoon and really enjoy himself. There is no better way to live one's relationship with God than according to His design in creation. Internally, however, the true believer will be unlike the other promenaders; his excursion is the deepest expression of his faith and of God's dominion over his life, while for others the walk becomes an end in itself (PS VII 482-83 LO 440-41).

To clarify this point, Kierkegaard uses a comparison with a day laborer in love with a princess:

What would be the humblest mode of preserving the relationship? Would it not be by living exactly like other workmen, by going to his work as usual and sharing the life of the rest; and when, while at work, he fell to think about the relationship, by admonishing himself with the thought that humility would please the princess better than anything else (PS VII 483 LO 441).

This interior ethics completely departs from ordinary human morality in which, according to Hegel, the external should always conform to the internal. Externally, the be-

[9] "Deerhaven," a wildlife preserve, nine miles from Copenhagen.

liever conforms to the prevailing norms. But this conformity in itself is not yet properly Christian; it is only a wrapper which covers the deeper internal ethics of the Christian.[10] No external act whatsoever distinguishes the Christian from the ethical nonbeliever: the difference consists entirely in the internal attitude of the Christian, by which he refers everything to God. Even martyrdom, so distinctive a mark of early Christianity, can never become a general rule in this new ethics, for no external testimony can ever correspond to a state per se internal. Christian interiority knows only its own unbloody martyrdom.

Besides the "universal" Christian ethics, however, Kierkegaard admits the special vocation of those who are called to be external witnesses for faith. Contrary to the normal mode of Christian life, they are required to testify outwardly concerning an internal reality. That was the special task of the Apostles and early martyrs: they had to propagate the faith. But no one may arrogate this exceptional calling to himself on his own authority (PS VII 496 LO 452-53).

This view of Christian ethics, which he defended until 1847, led Kierkegaard into great difficulty. It confines the specifically Christian element in ethics to a merely interior contact between God and the believer. By abandoning everything external, this ethic seems to place all social relations beyond the pale of strictly Christian life. But the Gospel undeniably contains a great number of positive precepts concerning behavior toward our fellowmen; its law culminates

[10] It would seem to me that Kierkegaard in his emphasis on the purely internal character of Christian ethics tends to exaggerate the distinction between the universal law and Christian interiority to the point where the former becomes a mere external conformity to the prevailing social habits, a sort of Kantian legality which is no longer ethical. In the *Unscientific Postscript* he even affirms: The only reason why a Christian cannot adopt the incognito of a robber or murderer is that the world has not degenerated so far that the open flouting of law can be regarded as the universal norm for mankind (PS VII 490 LO 446-47).

in the commandment of charity. How could Kierkegaard fit this into his ethics of interiority?

Some of Kierkegaard's contemporaries saw this flaw in his theory and objected that in his *Edifying Discourses* of 1847 he had nothing to say about the life of the Christian in society. That same year, he tried to answer their criticism in *The Works of Love*. In a chapter entitled "Love is a Matter of Conscience," he defends his ethics of interiority against the charge of indifference toward others. External indifference toward friends, relatives, and fatherland manifests as mistaken a notion of interiority as was shown by the medieval monk's external observance of silence; in either case, the *"mystery* of faith" (I Tm 3, 9) is abandoned.

Interiority is not indifference! A Christian never has a right to be indifferent toward any fellowman (WL IX 167 LO 117). The only thing indifferent to a Christian is the external form in which this concern for others manifests itself. In the law of charity, Christ gave us a truly new commandment. Love for one's fellowman existed before His coming, and He revealed no new way of realizing it. Christian charity has no external mark to distinguish it from worldly love; it is expressed in the same relationships between spouses, relatives, and friends with which the pagans were already familiar. Even the inclusion of enemies is not a decisive characteristic of Christian love, because love for one's enemies is conceivable among heathens also (WL IX 170 LO 119).

The novelty of Christ's commandment consists in drawing one's fellowman into the absoluteness of one's relationship with God. Thus the source of Christian love is neither blood nor sympathy, but God Himself. One's marriage partner becomes, first and foremost, a fellowman whom one loves for the sake of God: conjugal love is only a mode of charity (WL IX 164 LO 114-15). The commandment to love one's enemies acquires an original Christian significance only inasmuch as it is a test of whether one really loves others *for the sake of God* and not merely because of personal inclination (IX A 306) (818). Not the external form, but the divine foundation, differentiates Christian charity from ordinary love.

God's intervention makes love a duty. Although this has a sobering effect on sentiment and instinct, it implies no reservation in the act of loving surrender; on the contrary, by sharing my relationship with God, my partner acquires the same right to my love that God Himself has. Henceforth, this partner ceases to be a means by which I realize myself; he becomes an obligation to which I am subject. Such love is the opposite of secular free love, which is free only in being unrestrained. Christian love becomes free in being infinitely bound (WL IX 171 LO 119-20).

Earthly love is never true self-surrendering. "Love and marriage only confirm self-love more strongly, inasmuch as now there are two to be egotistical" (VIII A 190). As long as a man has not absolutely given himself over to God, he remains, despite all his good intentions and attempts to surrender, taken up with himself. Purely erotic love has its motive in personal preference, and thus remains enclosed in itself. In such love the other exists merely as *that which is good for me.* To be liberating, love must join me with another in such a way that the other is seen *as other* and not as an appendix to myself. Basically the erotic attitude is passive: it wants only to receive. Christian charity, on the contrary, is active: it is aware of an infinite obligation to the other. But the paradox of love is that only he who gives, receives; he who gives not, receives not. Only giving love enlarges and frees; receiving love encloses within itself.

The answer to the scribe's question, "Who is my neighbor?" can only be given by God. If I select my neighbor, then my charity, however reasonable, is based on my personal preference and not on my relation to God. Only God should decide to whom my love is to be given. Love attains its highest interiority when it is no longer concerned about the *what,* the object, but only about the *how,* the mode. In one of the chapters of *The Works of Love* Kierkegaard develops the theme: *Our duty is to love those whom we see.* Whoever God places in our path becomes of himself an object of love. Our neighbor's virtues or vices are irrelevant. If we wait to find someone "worthy" of our love, we may die without having loved at all. True love, on the contrary, *makes* its object lovable by placing it in a divine light. For when we realize that we have the same obligation to a man we meet in the street as we do to God, then every man acquires, apart from his human value, infinite dignity. The scribe's question, therefore, "Who is my neighbor?" is not the first to be asked. The first is: Who is my God? The answer to this question also defines my neighbor, for every man to whom I have a divine obligation is my neighbor (WL IX 33 LO 19).

Thus we see that love is not a sentiment, but a commandment, the greatest commandment of all, the "fulfillment of the Law" (Rom 13, 10). Only divine authority could make love into a commandment, for to the human heart "love" and "commandment" seem to exclude each other (WL IX 35 LO 20-21). Yet we all know that duty alone can make love endure. The human heart is fickle; the more it knows its own instability, the more it swears forever! But by what can a lover swear, except by his love itself? Yet this love can perish, poisoned by jealousy or extinguished by the infidelity of boredom. What pledge of love remains when love itself departs? (WL IX 44-49 LO 27-31). Only God's eternal commandment can save love from uncertainty, by placing it above the flux of the heart, in the keeping of the Infinite (WL IX 50-53 LO 31-33).

Being determined by the relationship with God, Christian

love also partakes of the infinite guilt which characterizes that relationship. Before God, man always falls short; that is why God's law ultimately becomes a judgment against man. Therefore, when love contains the entire Law within itself, it falls under the same sentence. The commandment to love my neighbor transfers my infinite guilt before God to my relationship with my fellowman: he participates in God's claim against me. In the face of this claim, man is always insolvent. The exhortation in the Epistle to the Romans contains the very definition of Christian love: "Owe no man anything except to love one another" (Rom 13, 8). Like my debt to God, my debt to my neighbor will never be liquidated because the two obligations coincide. Repayment against the divine claim must be made to men.

This essential imperfection of Christian love is also its perfection. The possibility of paying off the debt would destroy love. Even after heroic efforts, true love senses the distance between itself and its achievements; but this distance maintains its life and ensures its happiness. The very insufficiency which seems to diminish love, in truth guarantees it permanence.

3. *The Works of Faith*

Although in *The Works of Love* Kierkegaard still tries to interpret Christianity as pure interiority (and thus only reiterates the conclusion of the *Postscript*), the difficulties he encounters in his analysis make it obvious that his thinking is about to take a new direction. If one admits that Christianity implies a true ethic, one also must accept an external realization of it. Even in the *Postscript* Kierkegaard conceded that the highest ethical ideals, if never displayed, ultimately issue in vain sentiments (PS VII 370 LO 341).

From 1847 on, his work places increasing emphasis on the external realization of Christianity. Kierkegaard does not deny the pure interiority of Christianity, but he wishes to protect it against hypocrisy: total conformity with this world results in a betrayal of faith. In 1848, this is stated explicitly in the diary for the first time:

Christianity requires of me the interiority to renounce everything. But when I conserve interiority within myself I never reach the point where in a real sense, I renounce anything (VIII A 511).

Only one way leads to internal self-abnegation: to renounce something externally. So long as a person outwardly tries only to reap profits and to reach the top, all his pretenses to interior generosity are empty words. Over the years, Kierkegaard gradually comes to see the ethics of "hidden interiority" as a compromise with the world, which all but eliminates the severe demands of Christ. Christianity of this sort, thinned almost to nothing, is quite acceptable to the world, for this is the easiest way to get rid of it altogether (X³ A 334, and still more clearly in XI² A 301).

In *Training in Christianity* (1850), Kierkegaard criticizes the Danish National Church for making it impossible to confess Christ *before the world*. In a State Church we are all born Christians and never have to show our faith in Christ: to be a Dane is to be a Christian. There is no struggle; everything is so well arranged that there is no occasion to profess Christianity externally (TC XII 232-34 LO 205-07).

In *For Self-Examination* (1851) and *Judge for Yourselves* (published posthumously in 1876), Kierkegaard continues this criticism of "hidden," that is, inactive, Christianity. Finally, in *The Instant,* he launches an over-all attack against the official Church and urges his contemporaries to abandon its hypocrisy and disguised heathenism. Indeed, it is said that in the last weeks before his death he would stop churchgoers in the street to dissuade them from loading more guilt upon themselves by participating in the national religion.

This evolution in Kierkegaard's thought during his later years is the result of a new insight into the ethics of faith. If faith demands works, it must be manifested externally. Against the too-easy *fides fiducialis* doctrine of the Danish Church, Kierkegaard continually returns in his later writings to the theme: "Be doers of the Word, and not hearers only, deceiving yourselves."[11] Faith without works is dead. Christianity means new life and effort. But most modern Christians seem to prefer the ease of a dead faith to the effort of a living one.

Grace is generally taken to be a dead decision, made once for all; instead, it must tend to effort, since it is, to quote Baader, an *anticipation*. But to make an effort is always so difficult that in Christian life the most comfortable state is, in a sense, death, because then there is no longer any question of effort (X^2 A 223) [italics ours].

Grace truly anticipates only when there is something to follow. Without effort there is no grace, because grace is fulfilled only through effort. This does not imply justification by works, but it does imply *co-operation*. Indeed co-operation, although itself grace, does not dispense with personal effort. This ethical co-operation with grace becomes so important in Kierkegaard's later writings that they could be considered as prologomena to a theory of Christian ethics.

Christianity has introduced a new ethic. If the forgiveness of sin is a genuine *rebirth* to new life, it must entail fully

[11] In *For Self-Examination* Kierkegaard devotes an entire section to this passage of the Epistle of St. James, the canonicty of which he never questioned.

human *life,* that is, ethical life (X^3 A 182). As we indicated earlier, ethics is suspended, not suppressed, when it makes way for grace, and once the process of grace has been initiated, the ethical demands become stricter than they ever were before. Grace frees man only from the worry of saving himself by his own effort: his salvation no longer depends on this effort, but on God's mercy alone. The strain of the effort is removed—but not the effort itself. Without personal application, faith itself is dead. Man does not *really* believe if his faith does not permeate his whole life, since the surrender of faith is per se total (X^2 A 302). Good works are the symbol of a faith in which salvation no longer depends on personal effort. Free from all care, man can now employ all his energies in the task itself.

Kierkegaard compares God's attitude toward man with respect to grace, to that of a young master who succeeds an old lord. The old lord knew that his underlings could not handle the work assigned them. So he stormed and threatened when the law was not observed, but he let things drift. The young master, on the contrary, sets tasks which do not surpass anyone's capacities, but he watches very closely. From now on, everything must be in good order (X^2 A 239).

Sinful man is of himself in no condition to accomplish good; grace first enables him to fulfill his task. Once faith introduces grace, man must give it free rein in the works of faith. But these works receive all their meaning and value from the faith that inspired them: it is not their content, but the faith manifested, which is decisive.[12] Thus Kierkegaard entirely dissociates himself from what he regards as the

---

[12] Kierkegaard provides a new interpretation, based on the *sola fide* principle, for the Epistle of St. James: "When James says: Just as the body without the spirit is dead, so also faith without works is dead (2, 26)—one might rather reverse the order and say: so also works without faith are dead; for faith, apparently, corresponds rather to the spirit, and works rather to the body, than conversely" (X^1 A 457).

medieval concept of good works: instead of faith, asceticism was given primacy, as if fasting, almsgiving, entering a monastery, and torturing oneself were of themselves pleasing to God (X² A 181).[13] Through faith, man renounces reliance upon good works. Consequently, if faith without works is dead, it is even more true that works without faith are dead. The idea of these works is not that man, having received grace, should then *earn* his salvation:

Christianity asks everything of you, but when you have accomplished everything it asks besides that you realize you have been redeemed by grace alone and nothing else (X³ A 353).

To the end of his life, Kierkegaard opposed every theory of merit (cf. XI² A 301). To make salvation depend on works is, to his way of thinking, to reintroduce the impossible burden of the law. Good works are not a complement of grace, but its manifestation. Or, more precisely, the works of faith are grace itself, insofar as it restores man to freedom. The good free action is not to be considered a meritorious collaboration with grace, but it is grace itself which causes one to collaborate with grace. The will receives grace *as freedom,* that is, as a responsibility.

With the passing years Kierkegaard's viewpoint came to deviate more and more from ordinary Lutheranism, which he felt had abandoned free will by placing all the emphasis on the gratuitousness of grace. In a number of diary entries during the years 1848-1849, he confronts his own views with those of Luther.[14] Kierkegaard never rejected the *sola fide*

[13] Still, this notion has many advantages over modern Christianity, which only speculates and does not act. "The Middle Ages conceived of Christianity with a view to action, life, the transformation of personal existence" (JY XII 532 LO 201).

[14] Before 1846, Kierkegaard seems not to have read Luther. In that year, however, began an intercourse between the two that would be all the more fertile because Kierkegaard, by his whole outlook, was well

doctrine. On the topic of faith and good works, he explicitly professes the Reformer's ideas:

It is by no means human effort that brings about reconciliation, but the joy over redemption, over the fact that satisfaction has been made that leads to sincere effort. It is rather as Luther says: Not good works make a man good, but the good man does good works. In other words, the man is a constant who remains above all individual actions. And, according to Luther, one becomes a good man by faith. Faith then comes first. It is not by a life of virtue, of good deeds, and so on that one achieves faith. No, faith causes one in truth to perform good works (X² A 208).

But, already when he wrote the above text (November 1849), Kierkegaard realized that the *sola fide* doctrine with its reaction against asceticism opens only a limited perspective (X² A 207) (1003). It is to be understood as a corrective of the Middle Ages, when man fancied himself so meritorious in God's eyes that he could even transfer merit to others, or, if he preferred not to do any good works himself, could buy them from others at fixed prices (JY XII 533 LO 201).

Kierkegaard refers respectfully to Luther as "that man of God, who, with faith (for verily faith was needed for the task) and by faith reinstated faith in its right" (SE XII 353 LO 40-41). However, he objects to Luther's incapacity to grasp two opposed notions dialectically. Thus Luther neglected to treat of good works in his writings, although his personal life was imbued with them.[15] But no one ever

---

prepared to receive Luther's "existentialism." One cannot really say, however, that Kierkegaard *studied* Luther. Moreover, the spiritual climate in which Kierkegaard grew up was not Luther-oriented. The Lutheran revival in the Scandinavian Church was to come much later.

[15] In his private diary Kierkegaard sometimes sees Luther's life in a different light—he feels that in the last analysis Luther failed in his work by not dying as a martyr. But since this point concerns *the authority of the Reformer,* it will be dealt with in the next chapter.

recalls Luther's personal life. No one ever realizes he adopted the *sola fide* position only after tormenting himself for years in his monastery. Thus from good works Luther proceeded to *sola fide*, but the modern Lutheran does not proceed from anything: he is born Lutheran and is fed at the breast the superfluousness of good works (JY XII 534 LO 202). Luther's corrective concerning "works" has been mistaken for the whole Christian truth.

What Luther did by opposition—and, as it were, despite himself —against the fatuousness of a misconceived asceticism—that has become the absolute truth; although everything has become worldliness (so that the opposition has completely vanished) one keeps appealing to Luther (X² A 558).

Times have changed so much that today Luther would be the first to reintroduce good works in the name of faith in order to stop the word "grace" from being a mere pretext for refined worldliness (SE XII 361 LO 49).

Yet all the stress Kierkegaard places on good works never detracts from the *sola fide* principle: however great a man's efforts may be, works can never *merit* grace. Before the coming of faith, our works can only make us aware of our own powerlessness. And even then, it depends wholly on God whether this experience will ever become an authentic consciousness of sin; in that sense, our works do not even negatively dispose to grace. After the coming of faith, works merely *follow from* faith: they allow grace to bear fruit in the will, but they cannot be said to merit what they presuppose.

Kierkegaard's criticism, with which we are concerned in this chapter, refers to Luther's disciples rather than to Luther himself. The assertion that Luther denied the need for works is quite unjust. But certain of his pronouncements lend plausibility to this opinion.

Just as the heir does not work to gain possession because he
possesses already, so the works of the believer are only exercise in
act; as believer he in fact does possess everything, just as the heir
possesses the inheritance (IX A 22).

The works of faith are an overflowing of grace into free
will. God's bestowal of grace upon the will is the counterpart
of man's activity in the act of faith. Just as faith is man's
final act, so the assimilation of grace (in free activity) is
God's final act.[16]

However, if the assimilation of grace in good works is
still grace, how can it be a free effort on man's side? The
answer is that freedom itself is grace. It has already been
seen that grace can never be a necessitating agent, for that
at once would destroy the entire dialectic of grace and freedom by canceling one side of it. Grace can offer itself only
as a motive that attracts the will, without determining it. It
appears as an exhortation to gratitude for a salvation from
extreme distress. Thus the process of grace comprehends three
stages: first infinite humiliation, then grace, and finally an
effort at gratitude (JY XII 492 LO 165). But this attempt to
be grateful also is grace: grace in the form of freedom. For
this reason, a sharp distinction must be drawn between
Christian and non-Christian ethics. The Christian sees all
his efforts as a result of God's meeting with him in Christ.[17]
A Christian ethic, therefore, is essentially one of grace.

4. *The Imitation of Christ*

In the previous section we saw how Kierkegaard after 1847
gradually reached the conclusion that the internal attitude

---

[16] Cf. Thust, *op. cit.*, p. 368. "Final" must be taken here in a dialectical,
not a chronological sense, of course. Furthermore, faith is not exclusively
man's act, just as the assimilation is not exclusively God's act.

[17] Hirsch, *op. cit.*, pp. 861-62.

of the "ethics of faith" must manifest itself in the Christian's external behavior. He must become an *imitator* of Christ in this world. Kierkegaard thereby rejoins the centuries-old tradition of practicing the imitation of Christ. His pietistic background may have prepared him to reach this point of agreement with earlier Christianity. But it seems unlikely that his education did more than provide an occasion for personal inquiry, for in his diary he clearly dissents from the neo-pietistic Community of Brethren to which his father belonged. The Brethren, he claims, never achieved the true (that is, also external) imitation of Christ (IX A 362) (831). Only a serious effort to make one's entire life resemble Christ's deserves the name *imitation*. To be *truly* redeemed by Christ is, therefore, to impose on oneself the task of imitating Him. As man Christ is my model because as God He is my Redeemer. Christianity can be defined as faith (that is, confidence in the forgiveness of sins) together with a corresponding way of life, *imitation* (X³ A 454).

In a diary entry of his later years, Kierkegaard compares his theory with Luther's and describes the dialectic of faith and imitation very clearly:

Luther rightly arranges it thus: Christ is gift—to this corresponds faith. Besides, He is exemplar—to this corresponds imitation. But more accurately one should say: 1) imitation tending toward a decisive action by which the situation originates for becoming a Christian; 2) Christ as gift—faith; 3) imitation as fruit of faith (X⁴ A 284).[18]

---

[18] The first point was discussed in Chapter III of this book: ethics must raise us to a situation in which we become capable of grasping the essential Christian categories of sin and forgiveness. Kierkegaard can apply the term "imitation" to this stage of ethical striving only by analogy to his second form of ethics, or else, as V. Lindström (*art. cit.*, p. 383) claims, by an evolution in his own thinking about the preparation for Christianity. In his interpretation, Kierkegaard's earlier theory would have accepted as *given* the situation in which Christ appears to

Imitation therefore appears to be a derivative notion in Kierkegaard's theory of faith and, as he himself suggests, a continuation of the *sola fide* doctrine. For if forgiveness is preached without stress on the task it sets, then faith once again slips into a magical and extrinsic application of Christ's merits (IX A 79).

Christ is the Truth only inasmuch as He is the Way. He who does not follow the way also abandons the truth. We possess Christ's truth only by imitating Him, not by speculating about Him (TC XII 225-29 LO 198-202). "Christianity is not a *doctrine*. It is a *belief,* and corresponding to it, a well-defined way of existence, an imitation" (X³ A 454). Only in the imitation of Christ does contemporaneousness, this most important category in the dialectic of faith, receive its final, existential determination. By mere thought I will never be able to overcome the many centuries between Christ and myself, for I cannot forget what I know from history. Contemporaneousness is not attainable by speculation, but by the presence of Christ in my own existence.

Every true follower of Christ must, through his own existence, try to express the same fact: that humility and self-denial are inseparable from the Christian life (IX A 59).

The image of Christ which Kierkegaard proposes for our imitation is entirely determined by negative categories—from incognito up to despair.[19] Unconditional adherence to God in all things necessarily leads to a conflict with this world (X² A 317). There can be no compromise between the two—Christ's

---

the individual as Redeemer and example, whereas his later doctrine would have held that the believer must himself *create* the situation for the imitation of Christ by a decisive personal act.

[19] Mesnard, *Le vrai visage de Kierkegaard,* p. 378. Cf. also Hirsch, *op. cit.,* p. 884; and Thust, *op. cit.,* p. 329.

attitude is diametrically opposed to the world's. Persecution and suffering, therefore, are bound to be the chief marks of His life and the believer will have to imitate Christ in them. Christ's kingdom is not of this world—his followers will always be despised. Suffering expresses the qualitative disproportion between the Christian and the world (X^4 A 600) (1262).

But, contrary to what many people think, Christian suffering is suffering *because of Christ* and has nothing to do with the usual miseries of life, to which the non-Christian is equally subject.

To suffer in likeness with Christ does not mean to encounter the unavoidable with patience, but it means to suffer ill at the hands of men because as a Christian or by being a Christian one desires and strives after the good, so that one could avoid the suffering by ceasing to will the good (TC XII 196 LO 173).

However, on this point Kierkegaard's dialectic of imitation underwent such great development that its further course can be presented only historically. The *Gospel of Suffering,* written under the influence of the *Corsair* incident at the end of 1846, gives expression to Kierkegaard's first personal experience of the Christian's *opposition to the world.* In this account the notion of voluntary suffering, in the strict sense, is still absent. Suffering sets a task for the Christian, true, but only insofar as it is a gift (passively received) from God. The Christian's only duty is to accept this gift voluntarily.

The *Works of Love* (written during the first half of 1847) marks the end of the more passive ethics of interiority. True imitation, in the sense of voluntary *acting like,* is imminent. But with it the problem arises: To what extent is active suffering permissible? Does a man have the right to let himself be killed for the truth? Kierkegaard's conclusion is that a

Christian has this right only when Christianity itself is at stake, that is, with non-Christians. This solution, however cautious in its formulation, admits in principle the active imitation of Christ.

Ideas Which Wound Backward (written early in 1848 and published as part of the *Christian Discourses*) marks a new stage in this evolution.[20] Kierkegaard is forced to admit that the Gospel demands more than just a willingness, in an extreme case, to die for Christ; it requires an active imitation of Christ every day. "If anyone wants to go with me he must disregard himself, and take his cross day after day and follow Me" (Lk 9, 23). Voluntary suffering, then, seems to be essential to the spiritual life. The words of St. Peter, "Behold, we have left all . . . ," and Christ's inexorable demand that one hate one's father and mother, imply more than the readiness to stake one's life for one's ultimate commitment to Christ.

The Christian must bear witness to a doctrine that will inevitably bring him misfortune, and he must do this voluntarily. The paradox of Christian ethics is that its strict imperatives are given merely as *counsels*,[21] and while they are thus made tolerable for the mediocre Christian, they remain so high an ideal for the saint that he is never able to fulfill them entirely. Christ invites His disciples to leave everything in order to follow Him, but He does not reject those who fail to observe His counsel. The law of Christianity is the law of love, and love knows no law but the voluntary. But precisely

---

[20] That only voluntary suffering is Christian was first proposed in *Ideas Which Wound Backward*, but received definitive development in *Training in Christianity* (written in 1848 and the beginning of 1849).

[21] Kierkegaard is speaking here, of course, about the highest form of Christian life and not about the observance of the Natural Law. The latter is also part of the ethics of the Christian, but it is not specifically Christian. Only the ethics promulgated in the Sermon on the Mount can be called voluntary.

this voluntariness makes the fulfillment of the Christian law so difficult: love is never satisfied with what it accomplishes. No norm can be more exacting than one's own generosity.

Christian faith does not depend on human endeavor—only Christ could do what was necessary for our redemption—yet it sets tasks heavier than any human ethics. The Christian believes that all sacrifices have been abolished by Christ's coming, yet at the same time he is requested to bring greater sacrifices than were ever demanded before. Kierkegaard cannot agree with Luther that to *choose* suffering is to tempt God (X^2 A 263). He too quakes at the destiny of him who, wishing to be a martyr, yields and abjures his faith in the midst of suffering (CR X 213 LO 188). But he thinks that the fault of this man was not at the beginning, when he voluntarily chose what was highest (for then he only acted as a Christian), but at the end when he lost courage. Without voluntary suffering neither the doctrine of the Scriptures nor the conduct of the most authentic Christians, the martyrs, can be understood. This is not to elevate presumption into a Christian virtue. In his *Discourse on Becoming Sober* (1851-1852), Kierkegaard explicitly warns against foolish ventures undertaken on one's own initiative and only later committed to God's hands. In the ethics of faith no risk is justifiable unless it is taken *in accordance with the will of God*. This last proviso obviates all possible traces of presumption:

Just as no bird flew across the Dead Sea, so does no merely human foolhardiness get past this frightful understanding (JY XII 441 LO 118).

On the other hand, true Christian courage, which originates in God, is ready to act against all odds. Cowardice, or even worldly prudence, is irreconcilable with Christianity, and the worship of "probability" is as alien to Christianity as murder or theft. The man who walks soberly in the eyes of the world is so intoxicated as to be incapable of seeing the deeper reality of faith, whereas the Apostles who seemed to be drunk on Pentecost, were in fact manifesting extreme sobriety—before God (JY XII 442-43 LO 120).

Nevertheless, there still remains a fundamental disparity between Christ, who *freely* chose death, and His followers who never go so far. Must not this disparity also disappear? Kierkegaard's answer, formulated in the diary of 1848, was negative. Christ's life has been given us for imitation, but His death only for reconciliation. It would be presumption to imitate Him in dying too, unless one had been personally chosen for this exceptional vocation.[22]

Christ's death is in fact not a task to be imitated, but the Redemption. . . . Thus, it is not enough to say that Christ is the model and that we only need imitate Him. In the first place, I need His assistance in order to be like Him; and in the second place, inasmuch as He is the Savior and the Redeemer of humanity, I assuredly cannot imitate Him (X¹ A 132).

Christ is much more to us than merely a model for Christian ethics. As God, He is beyond all imitation, and in this sense only adoration and a feeling of dependence are suitable attitudes for us (X¹ A 134) (887). Suffering, humiliation, and self-abnegation are necessary, true, but by themselves they never contribute to a relation whose term transcends all human striving. In 1852, when Kierkegaard felt that his final great effort was required and he was himself on the verge of

---

[22] Kierkegaard's view at this time is that only the witness with authority (the apostle, the priest) can claim such a special vocation. Later, as we will see in Chapter VI, Section 3, he will assert that, because of the degradation of the Church, Christianity needs witnesses who without, and even against, the established authority stake their lives for the message of the Gospel.

launching a struggle which might cost him his life, he warned
once more against temerity in voluntary suffering.

It is easy to see that this thought might be dangerous. If suffering
is the characteristic of the relation of God, then the individual
might stoically wish, as it were, to challenge God to send him
suffering in order to show that he can love God all the same. That
is presumption and as unlike the fear of God as is well possible,
since it is egoism which impertinently wishes to measure itself
against God (X⁴ A 630) (1270).

Simultaneously with an increasing emphasis on voluntary
imitation of Christ, he stressed the need for humility. Christ
does not demand heroism of everyone, but He does ask all
to be humble enough to be sincere. The purpose of the
imitation of Christ is to promote humility (X⁴ 446). Everyone must measure himself against Christ's example. In his
very deficiencies one achieves the mark: a state of humility,
in which grace can operate (JY XII 539 LO 207). We encountered this dialectic previously in the relationship between law and grace. But it continues even after the operation
of grace, for Christianity consists essentially in *becoming*
a Christian, and never, in this life at least, in being a Christian. Grace itself undergoes a dialectical development. With
the first remission of sins, life does not come to a halt; man
remains sinful and will also abuse the very grace by which
he has been redeemed. Thus there is a constant need for new
grace over and above what has been received. Grace is not a
foreign, static element, present once and for all, but is rather
the interior development of Christian life in its continuous
struggle with the world. One will always be in need of new
grace to compensate for that which has been forfeited. "For
grace itself, grace again is needed" (X² A 198). As only life
can restore life, so only grace can restore grace after infidelity.
For every abuse of grace, the Spirit of Christ bestows new

grace, lest one fall into despair (X² A 451). There is only one
condition, that one be daring enough to die to one's old life
in order to receive the new. Parallel with the process of grace,
the believer must continually strive for death and abnegation.

Kierkegaard believes that his dialectical conception differs
fundamentally from the medieval *imitatio Christi*. Medieval
piety was based on the premise that in the imitation of
Christ man's effort acquires a value in itself (merit). Kierkegaard aligns himself with Luther's position: grace is entirely
a gift of God, to which we can contribute nothing (X² A 30).
In contemporary Lutheranism, however, the "gift" had become an excuse for avoiding any religious effort. Even the
medieval notion was better than this. It had its loopholes:
many found it easier to take refuge in the saints who had
actually imitated Christ than to spend any effort at it themselves. But at least they kept the necessary principle in view:
the medieval Catholic felt that something was *required of
him,* and he did not try to evade the issue.

If I want to spend my life in pleasure and am conscious of this
attitude, but on the other hand, want to stand in relation to
examples that express just the opposite, then it is, to speak
humanly, naively touching when I try to change the examples
themselves into mediators of a sort, thus recognizing how much
my life deviates from theirs: this, after all, is still a form of
honesty towards the examples (X⁴ A 342).

In a way, this childlike attitude comes very close to what
Kierkegaard considers the essence of the imitation—humility.
Christ's law bears down, but its weight, paradoxically, elevates one to grace. The more the law presses upon him, the
higher grace lifts him (JY XII 492 LO 165). Thus the dialectic of law and grace returns on a higher level in the imitation of Christ.

What is written in the Epistle to the Galatians 2, 19, "I through the law have died to the law," corresponds exactly to the explanation I am accustomed to give of our relation to the "Model." First one must realize that the model is a crushing demand. But thereupon the model, Christ, transforms itself into grace and mercy, and tries to take hold of you in order to bear you up. But so it is that through the Model you have died to the model (X^2 A 170).

We already learned in the third chapter that Christ is not primarily a Consoler but a Judge, Who, by His suffering, handed down the most severe sentence that has ever been pronounced against this world (X^2 A 320). With the forgiveness of sin, this sentence loses none of its force. In fact, the judgment derived from the imitation of Christ makes itself felt only after one's sins have been forgiven, and becomes more severe as one's relationship with God becomes more intimate: it takes the form of a dissimilarity, where there should be similarity to Christ.

Christ's law recognizes only one norm, Christ's person, and only one command, the voluntary. But for this reason even the most virtuous Christian will never observe it perfectly (WL IX 118-21 LO 81-83). One never finishes fulfilling Christ's law. The distance remaining is infinite and increases the further one goes (X^2 A 159) (993). When the Christian has done what he can, he has no alternative save to humiliate himself and to appeal to God's mercy (JY XII 493 LO 166).

This consideration should not discourage us: Christ came into the world for our salvation, and it was only to create the necessary situation for the reception of grace that He became our model and example.

Whenever we must goad ourselves, He is the model—then we stumble, lose heart, etc., and He becomes love, which helps us and renews us—then again He becomes the model (X^1 A 279).

Thus the figure of Christ oscillates constantly between model and Redeemer (JY XII 487 LO 161). In his later years, when he was so greatly concerned about the imitation of Christ, Kierkegaard still found it necessary to guard against a one-sided Christology, which regards Christ only as model and forgets that He is in the first place, *gift* and *reconciliation* (X^1 A 246). Reconciliation should always be the ultimate consideration—not only at the hour of death, when all one's efforts will pass in review and appear unsatisfactory, but also and especially *during* these efforts, lest they degenerate into anxiety. The need for grace will be felt most acutely when a man realizes that he already has stumbled and fallen into sin and yet must go on striving (X^1 A 491).

Kierkegaard gradually integrated this soteriological doctrine with his ascetic theology of the imitation of Christ. As early as 1849 he expressed the thought that it would be cruelty to drive up the price of salvation for poor people who have to muster all their resources just to make a living. To them, Christianity must be preached primarily as the glad tidings of consolation and redemption. It is in the salon that it should be made difficult! (X^1 A 135).

To concentrate exclusively on the sterner elements of the Gospel is, in fact, to distort its message. Did Christ not also come to lessen human suffering? Did He not cure the sick, the lepers, and those possessed of evil spirits? Did He not give the people to eat? Did He not change water into wine and calm the storm? In all these things the "philanthrophy of God" is evident (X^2 A 86) (978).

Only through the firm belief that Christ has already effected our reconciliation, and thus that everything is accomplished, do we arrive at a true conception of imitation. Before we even begin, the contest is decided in our favor! (X^2 A 219). And we possess a token of this victory in Christ's death on the Cross. Whereas Jesus' contemporaries before the crucifixion might still have doubted their salvation, we know for certain that He gave His life for us (ED XII 305-06).

Now it becomes clearer in what respect grace is an anticipation. It is the opening of a new life which man must fulfill, but in the very fulfillment he must continually take refuge in divine assistance (X^2 A 223). God's benedictions are not limited to one, as in Isaac's case. Every grace has its instant, but God always has a new grace ready (IX A 35). Every new grace sets a new task; in its turn this makes us aware of our need for further grace. With this in mind, Kierkegaard calls the imitation of Christ the "situation" of grace (X^3 A 470). Only by imitating Christ can our relationship with Him remain a dialogue. Without this active imitation grace becomes a "thing," a kind of indulgence, a dead weight on the soul instead of a living relation (IX A 79).

Grace is a dialectical moment of Christian life. However, it can never be placed on a par with other moments, because it comprehends the whole *reality* of Christian life. Grace *is* divine life itself, insofar as it is a dialectical negation of sin.

VI

THE PROTEST AGAINST
THE CHURCH

1. *The Dialectic of Authority*

ALL THAT HAS BEEN SAID about faith can be summarized in the thesis that subjectivity is the truth, and that faith in Christ is the deepest form of subjectivity.

We have pointed out that this subjectivity is not to be confused with subjectivism, and that, indeed, it fosters the fullest objectivity. For the act of faith begins in a divine revelation. God's message to man so far exceeds the latter's capacities that it must be given to him by a higher authority. However, that faith is a *datum* in no way diminishes man's subjectivity. The dialectic of interiorization is not halted by the notion of authority. On the contrary, the authority of revelation itself is paradoxical, and, therefore, enforces, rather than weakens, the subjectivity of religious experience.[1]

We have already seen that the Bible cannot be the ultimate

[1] This is indeed so much the case that A. Vetter in his psychological study on Kierkegaard, *Frömmigkeit als Leidenschaft* (Leipzig, 1928), calls authority a creation of the subject for himself, a conception which would lead directly to Rudolf Bultmann's idea of faith.

norm of faith. The concept of inspiration offers no solution, for there will always be the problem of which books are inspired and which are not. Even Luther, who accepted the Scriptures as the sole source of revelation, was forced to admit this fact implicitly.

He himself supplies the best refutation of his own biblical theory; he rejects the epistle of St. James, and why? Because it does not belong to the Canon? No, he does not deny that. The denial was on dogmatic grounds, and consequently his starting point is above the Bible. This was certainly his opinion, since he only relies on the Scriptures before his quarrel with the Pope, in order to stand on firm ground, while admitting that he would acquiesce if they could convince him from the Scriptures. And that was quite right; for what he wanted to do away with was, of course, the rubbish of tradition, which they certainly could not find in the Bible (X² A 244) (1008) [corrected].

Grundtvig's solution, basing the integrity of the *deposit of faith* on the authority of the Church, merely raised a new problem. For it is not sufficient for the Church to become conscious of its own existence in order to guarantee the perpetual security of the deposit of faith. Is this the true Church, the legitimate heir of the Apostles?

As meaningless as it is to say: I am conscious of my existence, therefore I existed yesterday—just as meaningless is it when the Church says: I become conscious of my existence, therefore I am the original apostolic Church. This latter point has to be shown and demonstrated, since it is an historical question (I A 58).

The *Postscript* shows that such historical proofs are always approximative, and therefore insufficient to found an absolute authority. Kierkegaard never tried to prove the apostolic succession of the Danish Church. He felt that, even with the best possible result, the effort would have been purpose-less, and that the labyrinth in which thought is trapped on this issue results from the idea of authority itself, rather than from any deficiency in factual knowledge. If authority in matters of faith is essentially transcendent and must derive from a transcendent source, then it follows that it can never be proven. When it is said that the authority of the Scriptures, of ecclessiastical ordinations, of the preaching of the Word are all rooted in the authority of a Church, this does not imply that the Church *validates* that authority. She cannot guarantee anything, since she can never prove herself, be-yond the shadow of a doubt, to be authentic. A transcendent authority is to be accepted for its own sake.

Luther's doctrine is especially weak on this subject; he pays more attention to the content of the message than to the authority which warrants it. For him *was Christum treibt* (what impels toward Christ), possesses authority, which means that its source can be determined by examining the message itself. Here, the author has no importance—only the doctrine matters.

Christianity's paradoxical difference from every other doctrine, from a scientific point of view, is that it posits authority. A philosopher with authority is nonsense. For a philosopher goes no further than his doctrine; if I can show that his doctrine is self-contradictory, incorrect, etc., he has nothing to reply. The paradox is that the personality is above the doctrine. It is there-fore also nonsensical of a philosopher to demand faith (X^2 A 312) (1025).

In commenting on the case of Dr. Adler, Kierkegaard clarifies the unique position of authority with respect to revelation. Dr. Adler, the pastor of a country parish on the island of Bornholm, appealed to an alleged private revelation of his own; as a consequence he was relieved of his office by the ecclesiastical authorities. Afterwards, Adler published several books, attempting to prove the divine authority of the purported visions on the basis of his "inspiration of genius." Kierkegaard thereupon wrote a work on Adler, two fragments of which were later rewritten and published under a pseudonym. In one of them, *Of the Difference between a Genius and an Apostle,* Kierkegaard examines the qualitative distinction between the word-with-authority and the word-without-authority. In the former, the authority, rather than the content, is decisive. When Christ says, for example, that there is eternal life, He is saying exactly what some philosophers had said. And yet, to the true Christian His word means infinitely more than that of Plato (GA XII 121 LO 154). Similarly, for a Christian it is presumption to call His teaching "profound," for only the sayings of men can be profound; Christ's teaching is not profound, it is incontrovertible! (GA XI 122 LO 154). The same holds true in the case of an Apostle. Many well-intentioned apologists assume that to prove the truth of the Apostle's message it is sufficient to praise the depth of his writings.

This kind of thoughtless eloquence is quite as likely to celebrate St. Paul as a stylist and an artist in words or, better still, since it is after all well known that he was also engaged in craft, as a tentmaker whose masterly work surpassed that of all upholsterers before and since (GA XI 112 LO 140).

To seek traces of divine authority in the content of the doctrine is to judge God's message by human standards. Authority is "a specific quality which, coming from elsewhere, becomes qualitatively apparent when the content of the message, or of the action, is posited as indifferent" (GA XI 117 LO 149). This qualitative distinction is based on the essential difference between God and man. So long as Christianity is

regarded as a mere "doctrine," it cannot claim divine authority, for even the loftiest doctrine does not of itself manifest the
transcendent.

Christianity is not a doctrine, but new life. As such it can
be communicated only by existence itself. True, the reality
of Christianity becomes established only after it has been
received as a message—and thus a direct communication by
the word is necessary—but in order to be understood correctly the "communicator" must prevent the hearer from
taking a merely speculative interest in it (PS VII 347 LO
320). Now, only the existential communication bears the
mark of divine authority.

How, then, does God give His message authority? By making
Himself master of some individuals and subjugating them to such
a point that they become ready at every moment throughout their
life to do, to undergo, to suffer everything for this doctrine. This
unconditional obedience of theirs is the very form of their authority. They use the authority and appeal to God, but at the same
time they back it up by their unconditional obedience (X² A 119).

To become a reality in the hearer, the divine message
must first be alive in the preacher, who should be, not an
orator, but "someone who exists in what he preaches" (IX
A 240). When a preacher does not manifest the message in
his own life, he has not preached *in truth* (X² A 604). A
priest, who preaches the Gospel, has no right to give a talk
once a week and to consider himself a private person the rest
of the time; if he wants to make his preaching true, he is
responsible for it at every instant (X³ A 62). Thus every religious authority has two aspects: the divine mission itself,
and its existential realization in the person in whom the authority is realized. Kierkegaard expresses this distinction
when he speaks of authority "in the immanent sense" and

authority "in the paradoxical sense." The latter is per se an object of faith without any human justification, whereas authority in the immanent sense consists in the living of the message by the person who communicates it. This kind of authority is defined as "a firm and conscious resolution to sacrifice everything, to put one's life at stake for the sake of the message" (VIII A 416). Ideally, the message will be wholly transformed into existential communication, so that the speaker becomes an exemplar rather than a teacher.[2] When Christianity uses teachers and orators instead of ascetics and saints for its propagation, its message becomes fossilized to a doctrine and its authority evaporates (X^2 A 146) (990).

But the immanent moral authority is based on the transcendent authority of the message, and since this is by definition paradoxical, it is without proof. Kierkegaard saw this problem and answered simply that all authority is ultimately grounded in faith. The existential living of the message by the preacher is a sign, but not a proof, of his divine authority. The fact that the preacher has put his whole life at stake indicates that his message transcends the ordinary, quantitative differences between one doctrine and another. But it can never become a proof, for that would destroy the essential element of every religious commitment: faith. Authority is basically an object of faith; the signs merely exclude arbitrariness in authority. No apostle could ever give conclusive proof of his mission, for that would make faith impossible.

An Apostle has no other proof than his own statement and at the most his willingness to suffer anything for the sake of that statement. His words in this respect will be short: "I am called by God; do with me what you will, scourge me, persecute me, but my last words are my first: I am called by God, and I make you eternally responsible for what you do against me" (GA XI 124 LO 159).

[2] Cf. H. Diem, *Die Existenzdialektik von S. Kierkegaard*, p. 170.

Kierkegaard's explanation proves that the notion of authority intensifies, rather than ends, the dialectic of interiorization: authority itself requires an interior commitment at every moment.

If one says that faith relies exclusively on authority, and intends thereby to exclude dialectic, one is completely mistaken (V A 32) (482) [our translation].

Many a commentator has been led to regard Kierkegaard as a Catholic because of the absoluteness of his principle of authority,[3] but the dialectical notion of "immanent authority" shows, in fact, a definite Protestant tendency. For in the Catholic Church authority must be understood wholly as an objective institution; the subjective disposition of the person in authority ultimately is of no importance, because the institution itself guarantees the correct use, at least in essential matters, of this authority. Once the divine authority of the Church is accepted, the man in authority poses no further problems. No signs are required by which he shows his existential commitment to the divine message. In the Protestant conception, however, the institution of authority depends on the way in which the person with authority represents and employs it. In the Catholic dogma of infallibility, the "use" of authority is given with the institution itself. Indeed, in the person of the Pope the question of how the authority is concretely recognizable, is terminated. For a Catholic there is basically no problem of authority: wherever the Bishop of Rome is, whoever he may be, there is the Church and there resides authority. In Protestantism the attitude of the Church is less self-confident. She knows herself to be a community of *faith* and, consequently, does not claim an absolute, divine authority. Any claim to infallibility on

[3] Most notably, Przywara, *Das Geheimnis Kierkegaards,* p. 82.

her part would be presumption, for the Protestant Church never *identifies* herself with Christ as the Catholic Church does in the Mystical Body. She stands on the side of the believer, *listening* to a higher authority. She can teach only *insofar* as she herself anxiously learns the message. The *ecclesia docens* is at the same time *ecclesia audiens*. The listening of the Church is indissolubly bound up with her teaching.[4]

This is obviously not to say that the Roman Church claims to have no need of "listening" before teaching. Such a view would be in contradiction with the Catholic doctrine that infallibility is impossible without "listening" to the revelation and the Holy Spirit as He works in the Church.[5] But, as Bellarmine stated it, the listening is necessarily assumed in the infallibility of the teaching. Nor does the Catholic position exclude the necessity of *living* the message of the Gospel for those who are authorized to communicate it. But in the article on the holiness of the Church the Catholic professes that there will always be sufficient sanctity in the Mystical Body as a whole to prevent the message from becoming unacceptable, even when it is communicated by unworthy dignitaries. No matter how depraved a particular bishop may be, he is unable to jeopardize the authority which he represents. In the Church itself the authority is entirely *given* and requires no further dialectical assimilation on the part of the believer.

For Kierkegaard, the active living of the preached doctrine becomes a necessary condition for the correctness of the message. He never abandons the Protestant viewpoint on the question of authority.[6] In the *Postscript* he explicitly rejects

---

[4] Cf. G. C. Berkouwer, *Conflict met Rome* (Kampen, 1948), p. 46.

[5] Cf. H. Denzinger, *Enchiridion Symbolorum,* No. 1836.

[6] Exactly what we mean by the Protestant viewpoint is a matter with which we shall have to deal later.

the Catholic conception of Papal authority as nondialectical.

This leads to a consideration of the concept of *witness*. The successors of the Apostles have no criterion for their authority other than their own testimony, that is, their willingness to suffer and die for the truth. As soon as they cease to think of themselves as witnesses in their daily lives, they lose their authority *eo ipso,* for they no longer transmit a message that can be delivered only by existential communication. Only if one bears this theory in mind will it be possible to understand how Kierkegaard could attack the ecclesiastical authorities with such unparalleled vehemence. In his book on Adler, Kierkegaard had made a thorough study of what a person with religious authority, hence a witness for the truth, ought to be. From that time, the idea had preoccupied his thoughts. An 1850 diary entry paraphrases it:

What is a witness? A witness is a man who immediately supplies proof of the truth of the doctrine he is proclaiming—immediately, well, partly by there being truth in him and blessedness, partly by at once offering himself and saying: see now whether you can compel me to abandon this doctrine. As a result of that fight, where the witness perhaps succumbs physically—dies—the doctrine triumphs. The opponents have no such doctrine for which they are prepared to die. That is a continued proof of the truth of the doctrine (X^3 A5) (1091).

To preserve this notion of witness in absolute purity, Kierkegaard had always been careful in his published writings to guard against being taken as a witness himself, for he did not possess the necessary divine authority. Those who were officially assigned by the Church to preach the message did indeed possess divine authority, but over the years it had become increasingly evident to Kierkegaard that they were using the authority of their mission to betray Christianity. Their

whole lives were so out of harmony with their message that
they were no longer witnesses for the truth. Their message
had become untrue by their lack of existential communication. It had become a doctrine instead of a way of life. Instead
of being turned entirely toward God, as a witness ought to
be (X¹ A 235), they were interested only in the world. The
term "witness" was less applicable to these persons in authority who lacked Christ than to preachers of Christ who
lacked authority.

In his eulogy of Mynster, February 5, 1854, in the Copenhagen Fruekirke, Dr. Martensen had called the deceased
Bishop of Seeland a "witness for the truth." After a few
months of hesitation, during which Martensen had been ap-
pointed Mynster's successor, Kierkegaard published a violent
article in the liberal journal *Faedrelandet* (*The Fatherland*)
under the heading: "Was Bishop Mynster a 'witness for the
truth,' one of the 'true witnesses for the truth'?—Is that the
truth?"

Bishop Mynster, despite his deeply religious nature and his
irreproachable life, had been largely responsible for the betrayal of the Danish Church. By his whole manner of living,
he had "tried to present true Christian preaching (namely,
by witnesses suffering for the truth) as an exaggeration"
(*Faedrelandet* 2/18/54—XIV 13). His personal qualities and
great influence had only helped to confirm this error; he had
been the pillar who for a lifetime had supported the edifice
of the secularized Danish Church, and lent it a semblance of
respectability. And now this man had been called a witness
for the truth, in Copenhagen's cathedral church, by the nation's leading theologian. Kierkegaard had to react:

A witness for the truth is a man whose life is totally unacquainted
with all that is called pleasure. . . . But he is thoroughly initiated
into all that is called suffering (*Faedrelandet* 2/18/54—XIV 13).

Such a witness was not to be found in modern Christendom, and Bishop Mynster, with his "brilliant, scintillating career," was certainly not the man to play that role.

Martensen regarded the article as an assault not only against his own authority and that of the late bishop, but also against the Church itself, which here was attacked on one of the articles of faith: I believe in one, holy, universal Church. In the leading Danish newspaper, he replied to Kierkegaard:

Whoever accepts this article of faith also knows that in the Church there is a testimony of truth transmitted from generation to generation and that at every instant and in every generation, in the community and among the teachers, there arise men to hear this witness and to confirm the great event of Christianity in a living and personal way. Otherwise, the unity of the Church through time would be destroyed. But it is useless to offer such considerations to Dr. Kierkegaard, whose Christianity is without Church and without history (*Berlingske Tidende*, 2/28/54—XIV 384).

Whether this last statement is well-founded is a question we shall have to decide later, but in any case it is obvious that Kierkegaard is defending a quite different idea of witness and of authority, and that this theory is decisive for his concept of the Church itself. An examination of the function of authority in Christianity will make this even more evident.

2. *The Church Militant*

Kierkegaard begins with the Protestant idea that the Church, more specifically ecclesiastical authority, exists to preserve the message intact. The Holy Spirit awakens faith in the Word, and this is preached by the Church. This does not mean that the Church automatically guards the message in all its purity: it can fail in its task by falsifying the content of the message or, what is worse, by proposing the message as a doctrine. What the Church needs is witnesses. It will never be able to do more than to give testimony, for the necessary condition for understanding the eternal truth is created anew in every individual Christian by the Holy Spirit Himself. No more than this condition is given in human nature is it ever entrusted once for all to the care of any Church. God's grace reaches each man directly and individually; therefore, the time of Christ's coming is neither the past (the period of the Gospel) nor the future (the Parousia), as Mynster thinks, but the present. On our part, we must try to eliminate everything that stands between Christ and ourselves; we must become contemporaries of Christ.

For this reason Adler's revelation particularly interested Kierkegaard: whether true or false, it confronted Christendom once more with the question of Christ's contemporaneousness. Even though it appeared that Adler had expressed himself incorrectly in using the word "revelation," the essence of the question remained the same.

Most men in their religiousness are present at the most in a bygone time or in a time to come, but not in a present time. . . . But it is different with Magister Adler. He truly is shaken, he is in mortal danger, he lies (to employ an expression used by another author) over 70,000 fathoms of water (A VII B 235, pp. 192-93 LO 155-58).

In spite of the great confusion in Adler's works, Kierkegaard gives him full credit for his approach to religion: Christianity again becomes a reality in the present (VII B 235, pp. 196-97).

With this idea of contemporaneousness Kierkegaard dissociates himself from at least the usual Protestant version of the mystery of the Incarnation. As Oscar Cullmann has indicated, the Kierkegaardian theory here replaces the faith in the past historical fact of redemption and in its future final revelation, by a reality in the present.[7] It has been said that this *actual presence of the reality of the redemption,* necessarily conditioning the act of faith for the Catholic but rendering it impossible for the Protestant, constitutes the chief distinction between Roman and Reformation Christianity.[8]

In the chapter on grace, however, it was pointed out that for Kierkegaard the reality of the redemption in the *present* is essentially a reality of *faith,* and that the new life consists exclusively in a new certainty, not in the final victory of the redemption. For this very reason he so strongly opposes the idea of the Church triumphant in this world. His position is as remote as possible from accepting any reality as objectively given by faith; that is why we feel, despite his apparent deviations, that fundamentally he remains entirely within the Protestant tradition. God takes hold of us in our subjectivity and there alone creates the conditions for faith—that is what grace is for Kierkegaard as well as for Protestantism.

Because the redemption is a reality of faith which remains per se strictly *subjective* and individual, grace cannot be mediated by a Church. From an ethico-religious viewpoint, no one can be of any real help to anyone else (SL VI 363 LO 317). Christianity can never be "handed down" by others. In this respect there is no difference between Christ's contemporaries and ourselves—in faith, we all become contemporaries. We rely on tradition only for a small, historical *nota bene;* anything else would serve only to deform the message. The sole

[7] *Christ et le Temps* (Neuchâtel-Paris, 1947), pp. 103, 119.

[8] Cf. W. H. Van de Pol, *Karakteristiek van het Reformatorisch Christendom* (Roermond, 1952). Discussing Newman, the author points out that in the Catholic Church, in contrast to the Protestant notion of faith, "the act of faith is aroused by, originates in, and is directed toward a *contemporary manifestation* of the reality of Revelation in the here and now: the Catholic Church" (p. 258).

advantage of the immediate contemporary of Christ over Christians of a later age is that for the person who lived at Jesus' time, the possibility of unworthy, idle talk coming between him and Christ had not yet arisen (PF IV 263 LO 57). In matters of faith God can reach man only in a strictly personal fashion in the depths of his own being.

God speaks directly to every separate individual and the instant He speaks to him He uses the individual himself in order through him to say to him what He would say to him (SL VI 333 LO 292).

True Christianity has no history—it is always *present*. Whatever time has interposed between Christ and oneself weakens it, so that the entire *history* of Christianity can be called a progressive defection from Christ.

The believer has no right to expect anything more from his contemporaries than from his predecessors: before God man is alone. A Church, in the sense of a community of the redeemed, which as *community* establishes an ontological relationship with God, can only soften the shock of the individual meeting with God (IX A 315). The realization that Christ, the God-man, has the personal love of a bridegroom for each soul places a heavy responsibility on the Christian. So what does he do? He brings the Church into this relationship: the *Church* becomes the bride of Christ. Thus it happens that a Church of nineteen centuries and millions of members faces Christ; this suggests that the two parties are on an equal footing, and removes the scandal of Christ's incomprehensible love for an individual man (X² A 231). The true Christian should try to eliminate this mediation of the Church between himself and Christ, in order to come face to face with God in complete solitude.

Kierkegaard feels that this solitude is precisely what Protestantism had to bring to the world, but that man's mediocrity was unable to bear it.

There are after all few men equal to bearing the Protestant view of life, and if it is really to be a source of strength to the average man it must either constitute itself into a smaller community (separation, conventicles etc.), or become more like Catholicism, so as in both cases to promote a communal bearing of the burden of life in society, which only the most gifted individuals can afford to be without (II A 223) (192).

For the same reason he contends that Luther could never have become a popular figure, whereas the Pope did: Protestantism is too difficult for the masses.

There can be no question in this world of a real Christian "community" which, as a community, is redeemed and sanctified. Indeed, as long as a man is in this life he groans with all creation under the burden of sin. Only in the depths of his *heart d*oes he hear the promise of redemption, and by faith in this redemption he is saved. But it would be premature to apply this promise as an accomplished fact to all creation. The "redeemed community" does not yet exist. Kierkegaard develops this idea in *Training in Christianity*.

Such a conception as that of "the congregation" about which people in these days especially have been so busy, is really, as applied to this life, an impatient anticipation of eternity. . . . "The congregation" therefore belongs properly to eternity; "the congregation" is at rest what the individual is in unrest. But this life is precisely the time of testing, the time of unrest, hence "the congregation" has not its abiding place in time but only in eternity, where it is the assembly at rest of all the individuals who stood the test of combat and probation (TC XII 246-47 LO 217-18; cf. also IX A 450).

In heaven there is an ontological community; in the Church militant there are only individuals (X^2 A 366). Instead of a Church which forms Christians, Kierkegaard recog-

nizes only individual Christians who in their individual faith
form a Church. The personal relationship with God is prior
to the Christian community.

The individual is first related to God and only secondarily to
the community: the first relation is the highest, although he must
not despise the second (VII A 20).

God comes into contact with us only as individuals. This is
why the Church cannot establish itself in the certitude of
God's grace. Grace does not exist in any human community;
it is limited to the unique meeting of God and the person.

If, nevertheless, a community does arise, it can only be on
the basis of each individual's certainty that he has rejected
the world. There is formed a small group of outlaws, having
nothing intrinsically in common but resistance to the world.
Its members are characterized by their antagonistic attitude
toward every other community. Only in this sort of "crimi-
nals'" conventicle does Kierkegaard see the realization of
the true Church (X^2 A 478). Like the real mother in the
story of Solomon's judgment, such a Church will prefer to
yield her children whole to others, rather than keeping half
of them for herself (X^3 A 54).

When Kierkegaard sees the Church as a community of
those who *believe* in Christ, he remains faithful to the
Reformation. The community is real inasmuch as it safe-
guards the Word, the object of faith, and administers the
sacraments, the symbols of faith. Yet for the individual, in
his personal life of faith, the bond with the Church is not
ontologically constitutive. It remains external. One should
not conclude that the Church is no true community; but
simply that it is not based, as is the Catholic Church, on a
new common *life*. In the above-quoted passage (VII A 20)
Kierkegaard points out that the relation to the community

is not to be despised, although it is of secondary importance. The act of faith proper is exclusively between God and the individual, but in order to elicit it the believer always has to rely, for the historical *nota bene,* on a tradition guaranteed by God Himself. Kierkegaard also believes in the sacraments as tokens of God's presence, to be administered by the Church. But he is very much opposed to any bond uniting the faithful in a mystical Body of Christ. Indeed, to accept such a theory would be to abandon the principle of subjectivity. It would also diminish one's personal responsibility before God and leave the way open for indulgences and automatic merits, obtainable by the believer only through a mystical union with the entire Church.

How did Thomas Aquinas, the greatest thinker of the Middle Ages, defend indulgences? By the doctrine of the Church considered as a Mystical Body, in which as in a party game, we all have our share in the kitty of the Church (X^4 A 369).

As soon as four shillings can pay off our sins at the debit of the spiritual community, religion becomes ridiculous (PS VII 515 LO 467).

The practical conclusion of Kierkegaard's conception is obvious. If we are essentially alone before God, it is immoral to engage in the salvation of others without a special mission thereto, for that would imply that God needs man for the redemption of man (PS VII 121 LO 122). Only the Apostles and their successors in the Church have been assigned the paradoxical task of working for something that depends exclusively on God Himself, namely, the salvation of others. They alone have the right to display certainty for others, even though they have never completely mastered the uncertainty within themselves (PS VII 496 LO 452-53).

The principle of subjectivity, as well as his own psychologi-

cal disposition and the romanticism of his age, led Kierkegaard to an almost complete spiritual atomism. The person,
for him, is a strictly individual category (VII A 70). Man is
distinguished from the animal in that the individual is superior to the race, while the animal is subordinate to its
species (X^2 A 489). Every man's existence is in his own hands.
For Kierkegaard there can be no "objective spirit"; man does
not require the mediation of the community, as in Hegel,
to become spirit. "It is really the conscience which constitutes
a personality. Personality is an individual decision" (VII A
10) (560). To become spirit man must become an *individual*,
isolated from the mass.

Modern man lives in an age in which all the ancient ties of
authority have been loosened. The religious world order has
disappeared; in its place there are only a number of nameless
powers, in which the hand of God can no longer be recognized. In this spiritual emptiness, man is searching for an
Archimedean point whereby he may restore meaning to this
world. Unable to locate this point within himself, he looks
to others for inner certitude. This is the origin of the form-
less, mindless mass which, as public opinion, creates itself
a surrogate for conscience (*A Literary Notice* VIII 74-118).
In the safety of numbers man tries to combat the insecurity
of his spiritual isolation.

The tragedy of this generation . . . is that it has abolished the
relationship with God, rebelled against God, and has the idea
that the relations of men among themselves constitute the
supremely important thing in life (IX A 195).
Men content themselves by taking counsel with one another, instead of consulting God (IX A 117).

The mass has become God, truth, power, and wisdom for
modern man; it makes and unmakes contemporary life.
Everything must bow to it. Relations with God, and with

ne's fellowman, have become impersonal—mass relations
VIII A 540). Like Socrates, Kierkegaard wants man to re-
liscover himself as an individual, and to free himself from
he mass (VIII A 23) (638) (VIII A 538). The first thing to be
ought is public opinion which, by constantly assuming that
ight is on the side of the majority, systematically reduces
nan to mass man (VIII A 134) (665).

Although Kierkegaard's individualism is not limited to the
eligious sphere, it receives its ultimate significance from the
piritual isolation of sin and the subjective interiority of the
edemption. In a noteworthy passage, E. Przywara summarizes
he basis of this personal isolationism:

Vith the exception of the most interior interiority, which con-
ists in the invisible union with *God-alone-operating*, everything
omes under the "ratio peccati" (the indelible original sin). This
10st interior interiority (as union with *God-alone-operating*)
1ust achieve a continuous isolation, an isolation from nature,
rom the visible world of man, from history. Indeed, it must even
1olate itself from itself, inasmuch as a religious existence always
ends towards a state of rest and thus departs from the *in indi-
sibili* of the immediate act; such a state has reverted once more
1 something human, which is not God. Christianity is spirit
gainst nature, interiority against office and community, contem-
oraneousness against tradition, becoming against establishment.
ut to the extent that spirit, interiority, contemporaneousness,
nd becoming still mean something positive, they too come under
1e "ratio peccati," because all creation as such comes under it.
herefore they are religious only in the sense of a fundamental
egation, even of themselves, in so far as they are not God's sole
peration "in act."[9]

With this in mind, one can understand why Kierkegaard
ills "the established" an unchristian concept (X^1 A 407).
Iis Christianity knows no rest or peace; indefatigably, it con-

[9] Przywara, *op. cit.*, p. 67.

tinues the war against all forms of certitude, of acceptance o
the established. It craves no other security than uncondition:
surrender to God. That is why it can never be content wit
Grundtvig's attempt to find certitude in the Church: such
tendency is wrong from the outset. "The ridiculous thin
about Grundtvig is that he always wants to have certitude
(V A 95).

The true Church knows no peace; it is militant, whic
means that it is continuously at war with the world. It r
mains to the end a Church "in process." That is also wh
it must never be united with the State, for the latter basical
represents the established order—in opposition to this ord
the Church is in continuous unrest (X¹ A 552) (941).[10] /
soon as the Church begins to live in peace with things :
they are, she betrays her mission; instead of cleansing herse
of all the impurities of this world, she makes a pact wit
them. She ceases to-be-in-becoming and simply *is* (TC X
243 LO 206). Opposition to the world has yielded to gree
for conversions in great number. In her absolute purity tl
Church existed only at the time of Christ and the Apostl
And even with the Apostles error had already begun: th
made more conversions in one day than Christ in His who
life.

It is not difficult to imagine how Kierkegaard, holding su
theories, would regard the Danish State Church, which h;
identified itself wholeheartedly with the established order
society. One also understands how Bishop Martensen cou
reproach him, even before his real attack had started, f
adhering to a Christianity that recognized neither Chur

[10] Of course, this means neither that the Church should rule nor th
she should reject the State (except when the State interferes wi
Church functions), as Kierkegaard makes clear as early as 1839 (II
450) (285). It means simply that the two may never collaborate to fo
a "Christian state" (X² A 240).

nor history.[11] To Kierkegaard's complaint that the militant
Christianity of the New Testament no longer existed, his
readers responded from the same New Testament. How then,
they asked, could he explain the text "The gates of hell shall
not prevail against it"? If he intended to use the New Testament to castigate Christians of his own time, then well and
good.

However, this is something that he can do only with the faith
that the Church of the Lord stands where the Lord erected it and
that His community lives on—no matter how Dr. Kierkegaard
and others interpret the New Testament—and this even at the
very time when he enters the Church to bring the congregation
to reason.[12]

No, it was a mistake to use the Scriptures to attack the
Church, without first having affirmed his faith in the Church.
For the Scriptures must be read in the Church.

3. Witness Without Authority

This reply of the Church posed the problem of what
authority a protest against the Church could claim. The
protest against the established order is no doubt justified by
the Protestant vision of sin and redemption. But such a protest belongs first and foremost to the Church which preserves
the Word. However, when the Church herself is immersed
in the established order, can anyone raise his voice, even
against the Church herself? What authority can an individual
invoke against the Church?

At first glance, it might seem here again as if we were
dealing with the witness for the truth. But this is not exactly

[11] H. Martensen, art. cit.
[12] V. Bloch in Faedrelandet, March 4th, 1855, XIV, 384.

so, since the witness for the truth must be someone in authority, whether it be that of an eyewitness (an Apostle) or
that of the successors of eyewitnesses (the ecclesiastical authorities), or even that of a private revelation, which has the
same standing as the authority of an Apostle. But, he who
protests against the Church does not belong in any of these
categories. In a way, it is essential for him to be without
authority in order to oppose the authorities. Kierkegaard
explicitly acknowledges that he is speaking without authority;
he writes his most important works under the pseudonym
either of an individual who indulges in reflections on Christianity, without himself being a Christian (Johannes Climacus), or of a person who is a Christian of a very high order
(Anti-Climacus), but who for that very reason cannot be
identified with Kierkegaard himself (X^1 A 512, 517, 530, 557;
X^2 A 184). Neither does he claim private revelations. Even
if he had, it is questionable whether a Christian having revelations would be in a position to protest against the authority
of the Church, for he would be protesting against one authority with another and substituting a new tradition for the
old. It is in the name of the ancient tradition that the protest
should be launched. When authority fails to preserve the
message intact, only someone without authority will be
competent to protest.

But this raises the question of whether in this case the
notion of authority itself is not destroyed. Indeed, it is
obvious that not everyone has a right to preach whatever
religious theory happens to come into his head. As a rule,
then, the individual remains subject to ecclesiastical authority. But there are religious exceptions—those who are no
longer able, or permitted, to follow the general pattern.
Luther was one of them and, at the end of his life, Kierkegaard came to regard himself in the same light. Through no
fault of their own, they were both placed *extra ordinem*,

in a new relationship with established reality. M. Thust comments:

Who, then, has really been called? Only he who has attained true insight about an absolutely important matter, when all others are immersed in error. How does someone recognize that he has this true insight? Undoubtedly, by the fact that he alone discovers and knows how to eliminate a profound misconception which has come to dominate his whole environment. One has only to think of the Old Testament prophets such as Amos or Jeremias.[13]

But how can one be sure that one has been called? Supposing that one is sure, how can one prove it? The one who has been called has no other criterion than the certainty itself with which he perceives the misconception he attacks. Therefore, the mark of his vocation is to be found in total interiority—even less than a person in authority will he ever be able to submit conclusive proof. Such a proof is per se impossible, and would only compromise the authenticity of his calling; religion is essentially subjective and cannot be adapted to outward categories. He who protests can obtain authority only by staking his life for it. In time Kierkegaard began increasingly to stress the position that the only way of communicating a religious message is martyrdom. After long indecision, he reached the conclusion that this was to be his vocation. He met death with the conviction that it was the only means to make his message "true."

But here it is most necessary to distinguish two phases in his life. In the first phase, which included the greater part of his lifetime, Kierkegaard related himself dialectically to the ecclesiastical authorities; in other words, as H. Diem expresses it, all his actions were meant to be a necessary complement to the authoritative Church. Kierkegaard's writings

[13] Thust, *Kierkegaard, Der Dichter des Religiösen*, p. 532.

intended to bring about indirectly the interiorization which
was absent from the direct preaching of the Church authorities. This complement had become essential, because the
authorities had compromised themselves by their illicit asso-
ciations with the State and with philosophy. Kierkegaard
considered his role to be that of a "corrective for the existing
state of affairs" (X^1 A 640), a purely reflective office, not
requiring a special election and therefore lacking authority;
he was a new Socrates, who, solely by indirect communication, was trying to revivify the Christian conscience.

Christianity required a "maieuticer" and . . . I understood how
to be one—while no one understood how to appreciate it. The
idea of proclaiming Christianity, of confessing Christ, does not
fit in with Christendom—that is exactly where the maieutic attitude fits in, which begins by assuming that men are in possession
of the greatest good and only tries to make them aware of what
they have (VIII A 42).

His task was exclusively on the reflective level: to help
Christians reflect on Christianity (X^2 A 106). Kierkegaard
had always been on guard against being mistaken for an
apostle. Even in 1854 he could still write:

I am no apostle bringing a hint of the kingdom of God, and
possessing authority. No, I serve God, but without authority
(XI^2 A 250).

From a purely religious point of view, Kierkegaard had
no more authority than a penitent, and so was as different as
could be from an apostle (X^2 A 100). To preclude any misconception on this important point, in 1848, after having
published nothing but religious writings for some years, he
wrote the aesthetic article entitled "The Crisis and a Crisis in
the Life of an Actress" (X 363-90; cf. IX A 189 [800]). His

purpose was only Socratic: to stimulate thinking. But at that time Kierkegaard was already aware that this attitude could not be the last word in Christianity.

The communication of Christianity must ultimately end in "bearing witness," the maieutic form can never be final. For truth from the Christian point of view does not lie in the subject (as Socrates understood it), but in a revelation which must be proclaimed. In Christendom the maieutic form can certainly be used, simply because the majority in fact live under the impression that they are Christians. But since Christianity is Christianity, the maieuticer must become the witness (IX A 221) (809).

Modern man is so enmeshed in reflection that he can no longer extricate himself by reflection (with the assistance of the Socratic method) alone; greater force is needed and only a martyr can rend the web (X1 A 16). Here Kierkegaard clearly began to feel that to be consistent with himself, he might be forced to adopt another position and become a witness, not a witness who has received his authority directly, but one "who has gone through the process of *becoming*" (IX A 221) (809). In other words, the Socratic teacher who becomes a witness has not had his mission from the beginning, but rather has searched so profoundly within himself for the truth that, at a certain moment, "God overpowers him," and as a necessary consequence of his striving for the truth, he is compelled to bear witness openly.

For Kierkegaard, however, a witness is ultimately a martyr. He began to feel that what Christianity needed, in the present as in the past, was martyrs. But for the moment he did not consider himself sufficiently mature spiritually to be one himself (IX A 302; X¹ A 281). He was a poetical-dialectical genius, a Socratic figure, who without authority helped the truth of Christianity to manifest itself. To prevent misunderstanding by his readers, on the title pages of all his writings of that period he had printed the words, "poetical, without authority, for interior reawakening," thus leaving the real task to the reader himself (X¹ A 162) (891).[14] Nevertheless, the recollection of the painful quarrel with *The Corsair* made him wonder whether he might not be the "extraordinary individual," entrusted with the testimony for which modern Christianity had been waiting. But he dismissed this idea, because what he had been opposing until then had not been "the established order," but only the "universally human" with which every genius has to contend (X¹ A 92).

In connection with the case of Adler, Kierkegaard had raised the question of "whether a man has the right to let himself be killed for the truth." The conclusion had been negative: in relationships with his fellowmen—or, if he happens to be a Christian, in his relationships with other Christians—no man possesses the truth so absolutely that he has a right to allow others to be guilty of his death (GA XI 105 LO 130). This investigation appeared together with *The Genius and the Apostle* in 1849 under the pseudonym H. H. Thus, for the time being the matter was dropped; Kierkegaard was only a genius (X¹ A 351) and had no right to attack Christendom openly, however flagrant its abuses.

Meanwhile, the problem continued to haunt him. In the same year he considered writing a complement to the above-mentioned essay: whether a penitent (as he constantly described himself) may not have the right to be sacrificed for the truth (X¹ A 331). Here the situation is different, for not only would the penitent's death be testimony on behalf of the truth, but it would also be an act of penance for the sins he has committed and would thus point to his own relative-

[14] Kierkegaard calls these works "poetical" in the sense in which the Platonic dialogues are poetical, i.e. they avoid abstract teaching (X¹ A 338, also 337).

ness. Yet, once again, Kierkegaard's answer was negative. Although, owing to his nature and early education, he showed many evidences of being an exceptional individual, this did not of itself indicate any special vocation from God authorizing him to communicate Christianity directly.[15] Kierkegaard's function was not that of a direct witness but that of a penitent who reflects on his own sins and gradually receives God's support "for what he had begun by himself" (X^2 A 375).

Later in 1850, however, he concluded that it would be demoniacal to remain on the level of indirect communication (X^3 A 413). A man does not have the right to leave the interpretation of his message to his auditors; ultimately, he must take an open stand, because he himself is also "in existence." But since he was not to be a martyr, he thought it presumptuous to give this direct communication about himself and about the meaning of his work during his lifetime.

[15] As we saw above, the communication of Christianity is always indirect, the reason being that Christ himself, because of His transcendence, cannot be communicated directly (pp. 138, 191). Any communication of Christianity which is merely direct, consists entirely in an intellectual message and, therefore, reduces Christianity to one doctrine among others. However, any authoritative communication of Christianity has to be partly direct insofar as the existential communication here is based on a divine mission to preach and interpret the word of the revelation. Such a mission to be a direct "witness" is founded on a direct assignment by Christ (the eyewitness), consecration by the Church, or private revelation. None of these could Kierkegaard invoke for his case. This explains why he hesitated so long to speak out directly (that is, in his own name) about Christianity. The direct communication which can be given only by divine mission, answers the question how far the indirect (the existential) communication of Christianity is allowed to go. Only he who by divine mission is a *witness* of Christ has the right to give his life for the truth of Christianity, because in giving one's life one's existential communication ceases to be indirect in the strict sense of the word—it becomes an overt communication of Christianity as something transcendent and greater than life itself. Only in case of a direct attack on Christianity by non-Christians does every Christian have the right and the duty to recur to this direct form of existential communication.

Temporarily, therefore, his autobiographical work remained unpublished. On the other hand, he began to hint that his anonymous writings were themselves not entirely indirect. Anti-Climacus was a compromise between a direct and an indirect manner of communication: Kierkegaard had for some time contemplated publishing *Training in Christianity* under his own name, which indicated that its content was not indirect—and, besides, he had signed his own name to the preface (X³ A 624). *Sickness unto Death,* too, had borne the name of its author. Moreover, Kierkegaard came to realize that his indirect way of communicating mainly resulted from the fact that he had not been sure in his own mind about many problems (X³ A 628). By 1851 his thinking had evolved so far that he believed he was able to give his life in order to make room for the "extraordinary individual" who would serve as *open witness* for Christ.

To be looked upon as the Exception myself, no, that I cannot do; to me that would be to besmirch all that has been granted me (X⁴ A 130) (1191) (cf. also SE XII 359 LO 46).

Kierkegaard still pictured himself as a powerless poet, who tried to influence people by completely effacing himself and letting the ideals speak for themselves. All his efforts, therefore, were directed toward interiorization, and no organized reform movement could claim his sanction. In a newspaper article (*Faedrelandet* January 31, 1851—XIII 472-80), he delivered a sharp rebuff to the theologian, A. G. Rudelbach, after the latter, in his effort to detach the Danish Church from the State, had referred to Kierkegaard.

Then suddenly, in June 1852, it occurred to him what his task really was: he realized in a concrete way what it meant to say that the greatest thing is not to understand what is greatest, but to do it (X⁴ A 545) (1248). All his former reservations about direct communication had been based on the principle that a Christian has no right to attack his fellow Christians directly. But this presupposed that Christendom was really made up of Christians. Now it dawned on him that this was not so, and that the truth he had defended was not a relative, but an absolute, one: the truth of Christianity against non-Christians.

Then, if that illusion "Christendom" is truth, if the accepted way of preaching in Christendom is the correct one, we are all Christians, and the only question is to become more inward: then the maieutic method, and not to be known, is the maximum.

But supposing now (what I was not originally aware of) that the accepted way of preaching in Christendom leaves out something very essential, the imitation, mortification, conversion etc., then we who are in Christendom are not Christians, in which case one must stress being known (X^4 A 558) (1250).

This meant that, henceforth, Kierkegaard would wage open warfare against authority. It was no longer sufficient to be a dialectical "complement" of official Christianity; the combat had to take place in the open, and, as he had realized even before this time, that could not be accomplished by pseudonymous writings, but only man to man by direct communication (X^1 A 466). In Kierkegaard's conception of Christianity, direct communication of his message also implied that he must lay down his life for it. Only then would his communication become testimony, and acquire the necessary authority. Besides, to live according to the spirit of Christ's message is worse than death, and the instinct of self-preservation is aroused in the person who hears this message.

And in this situation, in which he has no control over himself, he asks for the death of the spiritual man or else throws himself upon him in order to kill him . . . (XI^2 A 279).

These are the last words in Kierkegaard's diary. But the idea that present-day martyrdom can also be unbloody had matured in him over the years. In ancient Christianity it had been a question of life or death. In the present, the witness for the faith is not concerned primarily with physical violence, but with reflection, and so his death is rather a martyrdom of mental strain and spiritual suffering (X^3 A 303). In a sense, this "martyr at length" is less fortunate than the other kind; with him the coming of the catastrophe is slow. He must rise superior to the established state of affairs and be attentive at all times to the ideal which the modern Christian has eliminated from the world. This task—Kierkegaard refers to it as police duty—is so heavy, because of the continuous strain, that the witness will finally collapse (X^3 A 511).

This was to be Kierkegaard's fate. On October 2, 1855, he fainted on the street and was taken to Frederikshospital, where, a month later, he died. He considered death the conclusion of his work, and confided a few days before it occurred: "I shall gladly die, for then I am sure that I have fulfilled my task."[16]

Kierkegaard was never a witness in the ordinary sense of the word—he lacked authority for it—but the nature of his vocation was to apply a corrective to authority. Because of his testimony against Church and authority he deserves to be called, like Luther, though perhaps not to the same extent, a "protestant"—that is, someone who protests. However, Luther's work of reform failed, and he never became a true corrective because, instead of dying for his protest against the established state of affairs, he created a new *status quo*. A

---

[16] *Efterladte Papirer*, VIII, p. 596. This was the first publication of Kierkegaard's diary. Later it was replaced by the much better edition of Heiberg, *et al.*, *Søren Kierkegaards Papirer* (Copenhagen, 1909-48), 11 vols. This edition, however, is limited to Kierkegaard's writings and contains none of the biographical data which one finds in the first.

protest in order to be true testimony must also be a martyrdom.

Luther really did incalculable harm by not becoming a martyr. . . . By stopping half-way Luther lowered the standard of being a reformer and in that way gave birth in later times to that crowd, that rag, tag, and bobtail of nice soft-hearted men who also, in a way want to do a little reforming. Item: he gave birth to the confusion of being a reformer with political help. The result has been appalling confusion among the highest concepts and the most dangerous demoralization of all, as is naturally the case when something so fine, so noble, so subtle and so delicate as the concept "reformer" putrefies (XI[1] A 61) (1304).

For Kierkegaard the essence of the Reformation, of "protestantism," is to be: *a corrective,* that is to say, a spiritual state which is dialectically related to the established order. A corrective must never become a new *status quo.* It must restrict itself to a purely negative function: to die in order to give *what is* new life.

4. *Kierkegaard's Protestantism*

Protestantism had an important purpose in the history of Christianity: it gave voice to the eternal Christian protest against the complacent corruption of the established order. But it did not have the courage to limit itself to this negative mission. It did not continue protesting, but simply suppressed the established order in order to replace it by a new one. Thenceforth, suppression became the norm of Christianity. And since it is much easier to suppress religious duties than to fulfill them, the new attitude met with great acclaim. In this process, however, Protestantism, which had come to purify Christianity of all compromise with the world, actually succeeded in renewing contacts with the world.

Lutheranism is a corrective—but a corrective made into the norm, the whole, is *eo ipso* confusing in the next generation (when that which it was meant to correct no longer exists). And as long as this continues things get worse with every generation, until in the end the corrective produces the exact opposite of what was originally intended.

And such, moreover, is the case. Taken by itself, as the whole of Christianity, the Lutheran corrective produces the most subtle type of worldliness and paganism (XI^1 A 28) (1298).

As soon as the Protestant principle ceased to have any connection with what it had been directed against, only a very weak form of Christianity remained.[17] Protestantism is necessary, but it has to continue to be dialectically linked with the object of its protests; in other words, the two dialectical moments, the existing order and the protest, must be mutually evocative.[18] If either one is omitted, the other loses

[17] Kierkegaard wrote the most radical statement of his career a few months before his death: "Protestantism is absolutely untenable. It is a revolution which was started by a proclamation of the 'apostle' (Paul) against the 'Master' (Christ). It may be useful in certain times and under certain circumstances. But if one wants to maintain a position other than that, it has to be done as follows: We recognize that this doctrine is a weakening of Christianity which we have allowed ourselves hoping that God will be patient with it. But instead Protestantism is preached as a progress of Christianity" (XI^2 A 162).

[18] This probably also explains why, in his published writings, Kierkegaard always spoke with respect about Luther and Lutheranism: any other approach would have led his readers into the same error that Protestantism as a whole had made with respect to Catholicism, that of erecting the protest into a norm. It was only during the open attack at the end of his life, after he had seen that it was his duty to protest, that he dared to write: "Protestantism is, from a Christian viewpoint, simply an untruth, an unreasonableness, which falsifies dogma and the Christian conception of the world and of life as soon as it becomes a principle of Christianity, instead of a rectification necessary at certain times and in certain places" (*Faedrelandet*, March 30, 1855—XIV 50).

its religious meaning, for this meaning is composed of a continuous positing and sublating of human activity in its ascent to God. Kierkegaard had reached this conclusion in 1849, but he had thought at the time that the mistake was attributable to the generations after Luther's.

The misfortune of Christianity is clearly that the dialectical factor has been taken from Luther's doctrine of faith so that it has become a hiding-place for sheer paganism and epicureanism; people forget entirely that Luther was urging the claims of faith against a fantastically exaggerated asceticism (X^1 A 213) (899).

Gradually, Kierkegaard came to believe that Luther himself had been responsible for the misunderstanding, having been unable to keep his attention fixed simultaneously on the two poles of the dialectic (IX A 192) (803); X A 651). Therefore, there must have been something cheap in his way of acting, that enabled him to win the support of the masses, despite the fact that they were by nature less capable of adhering to his principles than to those of the Pope.

I often think, when I look at Luther, that there is one very doubtful thing about him: a reformer who wanted to cast off the yoke is a very doubtful matter. That is precisely why he was immediately taken in vain politically; for he himself has one side in common with politics, which is also true of his entire position: not to attack "the masses," but a particular ruler.

That is why Luther had such an easy fight. The difficulty lies precisely in suffering because one must make things more difficult for others. When one fights to throw off burdens one is of course understood at once by very many, whose interest it is to throw off the burdens. And consequently the real Christian sign, double danger, is absent.

In a sense Luther took the matter too lightly. He ought to have made it apparent that the freedom he was fighting for (and in that fight he was on the right side) led to making life, the spiritual life, infinitely more exhausting than it had been before (X^2 A 559) (1079).

If this could be said even of the leader, the condition of his followers is far worse, for they have completely lost the profound intuition which gave birth to Protestantism.[19] Consequently, the net effect of Lutheranism is negative. Something of considerable worth was destroyed, and very little has come to take its place. Christianity was "democratized." The Pope was dethroned, and the "public" was elevated in his stead (XI^1 A 108).[20]

The strong emphasis on the spirit has, through a lack of interior dialectic, turned into a "syllogism of the flesh," of which the replacement of virginity by marriage as the ideal of Christian life, is an obvious symbol (X^1 A 440).

One might be inclined to think that, after this vigorous attack on Lutheranism and even on the principle of the Reformation itself, Kierkegaard was well on his way to becoming a Catholic. In fact, several commentators have defended the theory that he would certainly have switched his allegiance to the Roman Church, or at least that all his beliefs were tending in that direction.[21] Moreover, it is a well-known

[19] Besides, Luther himself has completely disappeared in modern Lutheranism; one has only to consider what a row it would cause if a preacher of our own day were to deliver one of Luther's sermons in church (X^1 A 403) (914). Furthermore "What would Luther think if he were to return at this moment and look about him!" (VIII A 403) (711). To the very end, Kierkegaard remained conscious of Luther's greatness. Cf. the beautiful passage in For Self-Examination (SE XII 353 LO 41).

[20] As early as 1835 Kierkegaard had been struck by the coincidence between Protestantism and popular sovereignty (I A 93).

[21] The first theory is upheld, for example, by G. Brandes, S. Kierkegaard (Leipzig, 1879), p. 239, and by H. Høffding, S. Kierkegaard als Philosoph, trans. by A. Dorner and C. Schrempf (Berlin, 1922), p. 167;

fact that Kierkegaard's writings did result in converting several people to Catholicism, among others his contemporaries H. P. Kofoed-Hansen, F. Ebner, and, later, T. Haecker. More recently, however, there has been a reaction by the commentators most competent in this area against the "Catholic" interpretation of Kierkegaard.[22]

Indeed, the principal points on which this view is based are untenable. We have already discussed Kierkegaard's concept of authority in the apostle and the priest. Perhaps more interesting from a Catholic viewpoint is the theory of community which underlies the argument in *The Concept of Dread*. In discussing the social aspects of original sin, he certainly did open perspectives in the direction of Catholicism. Kierkegaard's ultimate explanation of original sin is that every individual is at once himself and the entire race. Thus, mankind sinned in the sin of one man (CD IV 332 LO 26). From this theory it would follow that an elevation of one man elevates all the other members of the human race as well. If, therefore, God entered the human race in the Incarnation, the essential relationship of all members to each other would form the *ontological* bond of a new community of saints. To admit the ontological participation of all in one man's sin is to admit the same participation in one man's divinity.

It has been observed that Kierkegaard actually did draw this conclusion, in the notion of the so-called "second Adam."[23] In a diary entry written in 1837, and thus much earlier than *The Concept of Dread*, it is stated that the parallel drawn by

---

the second by Przywara, *op. cit., passim,* and by M. Thust, *S. Kierkegaard, Der Dichter des Religiösen,* p. 16.

[22] E. Hirsch, W. Ruttenbeck, H. Diem, and J. Wahl may be cited among others. Catholic writers also seem to be taking a different viewpoint nowadays—R. Jolivet and H. Roos are two examples. A good survey of the *status quaestionis* of this problem is to be found in Roos, *Kierkegaard et le Catholicisme.*

[23] R. Jolivet, *Introduction à Kierkegaard* (St. Wandrille, 1946), p. 187.

St. Paul (Rom 5, 13-14) between Adam and Christ is valid
only if all men are linked in the same "social" manner with
Christ as they are with Adam. Thus the individual can be
saved only by Christ because of his ontological connection
with Him (II A 117). The Church, with its treasury of good
works, would then be the expression of this ontological possibility of salvation. This interpretation is quite obviously
Catholic, as Kierkegaard himself remarks—indeed, it may be
traced back to Günther[24]—but in the context it is only prob-
lematically proposed, just as the theory of original sin in *The
Concept of Dread* was no more than an isolated hypothesis
which does not fit too well in the rest of Kierkegaard's corpus.
To the best of my knowledge the objective theory of redemption was never repeated, except in order to be rejected.

Another point which would seem to support Kierkegaard's
"Catholicism" is that he regarded the Reformation's spiritual-
ism as one-sided. This is probably a consequence of his
pietistic background. It furnishes the clue to his remark of
1837 on religious anthropomorphism: "People fight so
fiercely against anthropomorphism and forget that Christ's
birth was the greatest and most important thing of all" (II A
133) (152).

His notion of the "contemporary" has also been given a
Catholic interpretation. As we noted earlier, the reality of the
redemption for Kierkegaard lies in the present—on this
matter he is consciously at variance with Mynster (VII A 78)
(581). But the reality of the present remains essentially a
reality of *faith*. Stated in this way, his theory, despite its
emphasis of the present, does not deviate essentially from
Protestant doctrine. Indeed, an objective redemption in the
present is probably even further removed from Kierkegaard's
conception than it is from Luther's. The existential character

---

[24] Günther, *Süd-und Nordlichter am Horizonte spekulativer Theologie*
(Vienna, 1832).

of this community of faith is due entirely to the transformation of faith which seizes hold of its adherents and alters their lives. However profound this transformation may be, it is not a new "reality" in the sense of the Catholic doctrine of grace, but the individual realization of a *faith in* a new reality. It is for this same reason that the Church on earth consists only of *individuals* who believe in Christ and imitate Him, and the *real* community of saints can exist only in the afterlife.

All this leads us to the conclusion that, if Kierkegaard's conception of the Church cannot be called a traditional Protestant one, it is even less Catholic. Karl Barth may be right in refusing Kierkegaard a place among the great Reformers of the nineteenth century, but this does not make him a Catholic. We would rather be inclined to regard his dialectic as a consistent application of the principle of the Reformation. Indeed, in Kierkegaard we are confronted with a Protestantism which will continue protesting, because it knows that both moments, the existing state of things as well as the protest against it, are equally essential for the pure realization of Christianity. Whenever the protest suppresses the existent state, a new reality comes into being; against this, too, a protest must be made in the name of God's transcendency.

We question whether the real import of this dialectic for Kierkegaard has ever been sufficiently stressed. Even H. Diem, who deserves the greatest credit for having applied the dialectic as a universal principle of Kierkegaardian interpretation, did not draw the ultimate conclusions from this principle. That is why his analysis lacks a certain quality of coherence. He sees two opposed tendencies in Kierkegaard: the first, more in evidence in the published writings, aims merely to serve as a corrective of the established state of things and relates itself dialectically to the authoritative Church without ever opposing its authority; the second, apparent mainly in the diary references to Luther, would ultimately destroy the whole concept of authority in the Church and lead to a purely subjective approach to faith. Diem's study closes by posing the question which of the two is the real Kierkegaard.

But, as W. Anz has pointed out in an incisive article, granted that both tendencies are simultaneously present in Kierkegaard, the real question of the theologian or the philosopher is whether Kierkegaard's *statement of the problem* itself has not already placed him outside the Church. The idea of a corrective and the radical attack on authority (in the Luther entries) can be reduced to a common denominator, and the category of a corrective within Christendom already implies, according to Anz, the suppression of the Church.

Kierkegaard's absolute subjectivity transforms all that opposes it, which he terms the "world," into something non-Christian. Thus every historical fact necessarily comes to be included on the side of the world.

From the standpoint of the "Ideal" every use of grace . . . must appear as a weakening, a making relative or a secularizing of existence. And so the whole of historical Christianity is found on the side of the world, and is denied with the same radical one-sidedness as the world of antiquity, of romanticism, of history, or of the intellect.[25]

Anz concludes that, by its extreme subjectivism, Kierkegaard's existential dialectic is just as individualistic and destructive of any sort of organized Christianity as Nietzsche's philosophy is of the idea of community.[26]

[25] W. Anz, "Fragen der Kierkegaard Interpretation," *Theologische Rundschau*, 20 (1952), p. 62.
[26] Anz, *art. cit.*, pp. 71-72.

Is this the last word on the subject? Is Kierkegaard only negative? It is certainly true that the negative moment of the dialectical process annuls the positive, and for this reason can never be overemphasized. But it is never absolute, for then it would halt the movement of the dialectic itself. Therefore, the second moment must be followed by a third. The dialectical negation necessarily negates itself also, because it is only the negation of this *particular* affirmation. And thus it ultimately becomes positive again. The force of the negation lies in the fact that is not just negation, but sublation; thus each moment which has been encountered along the way in the dialectic is preserved. It loses only its abstract independence, and becomes subordinate to the whole.

This positive aspect of dialectical negation in Kierkegaard has not been sufficiently taken into account. That is why, in the usual interpretation, the final result is so negative that practically nothing is left of Christianity. Kierkegaard has protested against everything which is not the pure subjectivity in which God comes into contact with the individual, and in this respect he is more radical than Luther. But a dialectical protest is not like an ordinary protest that stands alone and becomes its own norm. Just because he was not dialectical, Luther could not go so far in his protest as did Kierkegaard.

The latter attacks everything. It is true there is not much room left for an established Church in the wake of his critical diary entries on Luther. It is even true, as Anz says, that the principles behind these remarks are not limited to a criticism of Luther; but it is also true that this entire critique should be read in the light of the whole existential dialectic, within the framework of which it occurs. That is why Kierkegaard's *Attack on Christendom* could be so merciless. It was and remained from beginning to end a *dialectical* attack, and, as

Kierkegaard himself once wrote, a dialectical attack on Christianity is ultimately a defense of it (X^2 A 163) (994). Or, more exactly: whether it is an attack or a defense will depend on the Church, and the way in which it takes it.

Therefore, we consider Kierkegaard's effort a consistent Protestantism. He is a person who kept protesting, who could never accept a Church which had become established, even if on the basis of protest itself. In most instances, the Protestant principle has been abandoned as soon as it has developed itself to the point of becoming a Church. Kierkegaard's intransigent Protestantism continued to protest; he protested against everything, even against the protest itself. Therefore his attitude was not purely negative, but made itself positive once again.

The question has been raised whether this negation of the negation would not bring him back into the Church of Rome again. We think not. For the Catholic Church cannot accept the dialectical principle except in her own bosom. Kierkegaard himself was fully conscious of this and, during the course of his sharpest criticism of Protestantism, made it clear that his position was far removed from the Catholic stance.

To enter the Catholic Church would be an ill-advised step that I will not take, but that people might expect, because in our times they seem completely to have forgotten what Christianity is (XIV 50).

As a matter of fact, dialectical Christianity is not the Catholic kind. It is true that Kierkegaard placed himself beyond the pale of the Protestant *Church*. But he never abandoned the Protestant principle. By his unshaken faithfulness to this principle he managed to adopt an original attitude toward Catholicism. His dialectical approach succeeded in re-establishing the dialogue with the positive moment, and that is why so many who came under his influence could become Catholics. But his own relation to Catholicism was dialectical: "an antipathetic sympathy and a sympathetic antipathy."

For references to Mikael Kierkegaard, see Chapter I, section 1; to Regine Olsen, see Chapter I, section 2; to Kierkegaard's pseudonyms, see *System of References*. For Bible texts cited, see below.

227